MERN STACK WEB DEVELOPMENT

CRACKING MNC TECHNICAL INTERVIEWS

MongoDB, Express.js,
React.js, Node.js

NIRM D.

ISBN-13: 9798313728933

Cover design by: Art Painter
Library of Congress Control Number: 2018675309
Printed in the United States of America

To the job seekers and aspiring developers
who dare to dream big and work relentlessly to achieve their
goals.

To the mentors and industry leaders
who inspire, guide, and push the boundaries of innovation in
MERN stack development.

To the peers and colleagues
who foster collaboration, share knowledge, and make learning
a lifelong journey.

And to everyone
who believes in growth, resilience, and the power
of continuous learning—this book is for you.

CONTENT

PREFACE

**Mastering the MERN Stack to Crack
MNC Technical Interviews**

- In today's rapidly evolving digital landscape, **full-stack development** has become one of the most sought-after skills in the tech industry. The ability to build **scalable, dynamic, and high-performance web applications** is essential for any developer aiming to secure a position in a **multinational company (MNC).** Among various full-stack technologies, **MERN (MongoDB, Express.js, React.js, Node.js) has emerged as a dominant stack** due to its flexibility, efficiency, and ability to power some of the most widely used applications today.

- If you are reading this book, chances are you are **preparing for a MERN stack developer role in an MNC.** You might be a **fresh graduate, a self-taught programmer, or an experienced developer** looking to transition into full-stack development. Regardless of your background, this book is designed to equip you with the **technical knowledge, problem-solving strategies, and real-world insights** needed to ace your MERN stack interviews and land your dream job.

Why the MERN Stack?

The Rise of MERN in Modern Web Development

- The **MERN stack** has revolutionized modern web development by enabling developers to use **JavaScript across the entire stack**—from the database to the frontend UI. Unlike traditional server-side technologies that require different programming languages for backend and frontend development, MERN offers a **seamless JavaScript-powered ecosystem** that is highly efficient and developer-friendly.

Why MNCs Prefer MERN Stack Developers

- MNCs across industries, from **finance and healthcare to e-commerce and SaaS**, rely on MERN-based applications for their ability to scale effortlessly. Companies like **Netflix, Facebook, Airbnb, and Uber** have adopted **Node.js and React.js** due to their **performance, maintainability, and ease of scaling**. Hiring managers in MNCs look for MERN developers who can:

- **Design and implement scalable full-stack applications.**
- **Optimize backend APIs for high performance** using Node.js and Express.
- **Build dynamic, high-performance user interfaces** using React.js.
- **Efficiently manage databases** with MongoDB for real-world applications.
- By mastering the **MERN stack**, you position yourself as a **highly valuable asset to top-tier companies**, making yourself eligible for **high-paying web development roles** worldwide.

Common Challenges in MERN Stack Technical Interviews

- Landing a **MERN stack developer job at an MNC** is **not just about knowing the technology**—it's about demonstrating **problem-solving ability, system design expertise, and coding efficiency** under pressure. Many candidates struggle with:
- **Mastering Full-Stack Concepts** – Balancing frontend, backend, and database knowledge.
- **Handling Real-World Coding Challenges** – Implementing optimized, scalable, and maintainable solutions.
- **Optimizing APIs and Queries** – Writing efficient backend logic and MongoDB queries.
- **Building High-Performance React Applications** – Managing state effectively and improving rendering performance.
- **Scaling Applications for High Traffic** – Designing robust architectures that handle millions of users.
- **Performing Well in System Design Interviews** – Structuring applications for scalability and fault tolerance.
- **Excelling in Behavioral and HR Interviews** – Showcasing teamwork, leadership, and problem-solving skills.

How This Book Helps You Overcome These Challenges

- This book is structured to **bridge the gap between theory and real-world application**. It does not just cover the **fundamentals of MERN stack development**, but also **teaches you how to apply these concepts in MNC-level interviews**. The book takes a **step-by-step approach**, focusing on both **technical depth and interview readiness**.

How This Book Is Structured

- This book is divided into **expertly crafted sections** that cover **every critical aspect of MERN stack development and interview preparation**.

1. Mastering the Core MERN Stack Technologies

- We begin with an in-depth exploration of **each component of the MERN stack:**
- **MongoDB Essentials** – Designing schemas, indexing strategies, querying large datasets, and optimizing database performance.
- **Express.js Fundamentals** – Building RESTful APIs, middleware implementation, authentication, and security best practices.
- **React.js for MNC Interviews** – Writing optimized React code, handling state management, and improving rendering performance.
- **Node.js Deep Dive** – Understanding event-driven architecture, managing concurrency, and debugging Node.js applications.

2. Tackling Real-World MERN Stack Challenges

- MNCs assess candidates based on their ability to **solve real-world full-stack problems**. This book covers:
- **Building authentication systems (JWT, OAuth).**
- **Optimizing API response times and caching strategies.**

- Implementing scalable pagination and filtering in MongoDB.
- Building real-time applications using WebSockets and Socket.io.
- Implementing secure file uploads with AWS S3 and Cloudinary.
- Each problem is **broken down step-by-step**, with **optimized solutions, best practices, and common pitfalls to avoid.**

3. System Design and Scalability for MERN Applications

- For senior-level positions, MNCs test **system design** expertise. This book includes:
- **Designing large-scale MERN applications** with high availability.
- **Horizontal vs. vertical scaling approaches.**
- **Microservices vs. monolithic architecture decisions.**
- **Load balancing, database sharding, and caching techniques.**

4. Coding Challenges and Algorithmic Thinking

- Coding proficiency is tested in every **MNC technical interview**. This book includes:
- **Data structures and algorithms relevant to full-stack development.**
- **Common coding problems with optimized solutions.**
- **Time complexity analysis for improving performance.**

5. Behavioral and HR Interviews

- Technical skills alone **won't land you the job**—you need to **communicate effectively** and fit into the company culture. This book provides:
- **15+ common behavioral interview questions** with sample answers.
- **Strategies to answer leadership, teamwork, and conflict-resolution questions.**

- **Salary negotiation techniques** and handling job offers.

Why This Book Is Different

Unlike generic programming books, this book is:

- **Tailored for MNC-Level Interviews** – It provides **real-world problems** that companies like Amazon, Google, and Facebook ask.
- **Highly Practical and Hands-On** – Includes **step-by-step implementations, best practices, and real-world scenarios**.
- **Optimized for Different Experience Levels** – Whether you're a **junior developer or a senior engineer**, this book adapts to your needs.
- **Focused on Industry Standards** – Covers **code optimization, security best practices, and system scalability**.

A Motivational Note for Developers

- Becoming a **successful MERN stack developer at an MNC** requires more than just knowledge—it requires **dedication, practice, and continuous learning**. Every **coding challenge, failed interview, and debugging struggle** is an opportunity to grow.
- **For freshers**, this book provides a **structured path** to breaking into the industry.
- **For experienced developers**, this book helps you **level up and tackle system design challenges confidently**.

Continuous Learning in Web Development

- Technology evolves **rapidly**—what is relevant today may become obsolete tomorrow. **MERN stack development is no exception.** The best developers are those who:
- **Stay updated with the latest trends (React Server**

Components, Edge Functions, Microservices).

- **Contribute to open-source projects** and build a personal brand.
- **Engage with developer communities** on GitHub, Stack Overflow, and LinkedIn.
- This book is **not just a guide for cracking interviews— it's a long-term resource** to help you **grow as a MERN stack developer throughout your career.**

Final Thoughts

- Mastering the MERN stack and securing an MNC job is **achievable with the right preparation strategy.** This book provides everything you need to:
- **Build strong technical foundations** in MongoDB, Express, React, and Node.
- **Solve real-world coding challenges** with confidence.
- **Design scalable and high-performance applications.**
- **Communicate effectively** and ace behavioral interviews.

CHAPTER 1

Introduction to MERN Stack Interviews

Overview of the MERN Stack

- The MERN stack—comprising **MongoDB, Express.js, React, and Node.js**—is a powerful and widely used technology stack for full-stack web development. It enables developers to build scalable, high-performance applications using a **JavaScript-based ecosystem**, making it a preferred choice for both startups and multinational companies (MNCs).

What is the MERN Stack?

- **MongoDB**: A NoSQL database that stores data in JSON-like documents, offering flexibility and scalability.
- **Express.js**: A lightweight and efficient web application framework for Node.js, simplifying backend development.
- **React.js**: A JavaScript library for building dynamic and interactive user interfaces.
- **Node.js**: A runtime environment that allows JavaScript to run on the server side, enabling full-stack development with a single language.

Why is MERN Popular for Full-Stack Development?

- **Unified JavaScript Ecosystem**: MERN allows developers to use JavaScript/TypeScript throughout the stack, reducing context-switching and improving efficiency.

- **Scalability and Performance**: With a non-blocking, event-driven architecture, Node.js and MongoDB enable applications to handle large-scale data and high user traffic.
- **Rich Community Support**: Being open-source and widely adopted, MERN benefits from a vast community, extensive libraries, and continuous updates.
- **Flexibility**: The MERN stack supports both **monolithic** and **microservices architectures**, making it adaptable to different project needs.

Real-World Applications of MERN Stack in MNCs

Many leading multinational companies use the MERN stack for various applications, including:

- **E-commerce Platforms** (e.g., Amazon-like marketplaces)
- **Social Media Applications** (e.g., real-time chat applications and content-sharing platforms)
- **Enterprise Resource Planning (ERP) Systems**
- **FinTech Solutions** (e.g., digital banking dashboards, fraud detection systems)
- **Content Management Systems (CMS)** (e.g., headless CMS for dynamic websites)
- **Healthcare Applications** (e.g., telemedicine platforms, electronic health records)
- **Educational Platforms** (e.g., online learning management systems)
- **Project Management Tools** (e.g., Trello-like task management apps)

What MNCs Look for in a MERN Stack Developer

- Landing a MERN stack developer role in an MNC requires a well-rounded skill set beyond just coding. Companies seek professionals who can build **scalable, secure, and high-performance applications** while collaborating with cross-functional teams.

Key Skills and Experience Required

- **Frontend Expertise**: Proficiency in React.js, state management (Redux/Zustand), and component-based architecture.
- **Backend Development**: Strong knowledge of Node.js, Express.js, authentication (JWT, OAuth), and RESTful/ GraphQL APIs.
- **Database Management**: Understanding MongoDB schemas, indexing, aggregation pipelines, and performance optimization.
- **Version Control**: Familiarity with Git/GitHub workflows.
- **Deployment and DevOps**: Experience with CI/CD pipelines, cloud platforms (AWS, Azure), and containerization (Docker, Kubernetes).
- **Soft Skills**: Problem-solving, teamwork, and effective communication are crucial for working in large-scale enterprise environments.

Importance of Problem-Solving, System Design, and Coding Proficiency

- **Problem-Solving**: MNCs evaluate logical thinking and algorithmic efficiency through data structures and algorithms (DSA) challenges.
- **System Design**: Understanding architectural patterns, scalability strategies, and API design principles is essential.
- **Coding Proficiency**: Strong hands-on experience in JavaScript, TypeScript, and testing frameworks (Jest, Mocha) is required.

Role of MERN Developers in Modern Web Applications

MERN developers play a crucial role in building and maintaining enterprise-level applications, often handling tasks such as:

- **Developing dynamic UIs with React**
- **Designing and optimizing APIs using Express.js**

- Integrating databases and ensuring data integrity with MongoDB
- Managing authentication, security, and performance optimizations

Common Interview Formats and Question Types

MNCs follow a structured interview process to assess MERN stack candidates, typically consisting of multiple rounds:

Stages of MERN Stack Interviews

- **Initial Screening**: HR assesses resume, experience, and basic technical skills.
- **Technical Rounds**: In-depth coding tests, problem-solving, and system design discussions.
- **System Design Interview**: Evaluates knowledge of scalable architectures and best practices.
- **HR and Cultural Fit Round**: Assesses communication skills, teamwork, and company alignment.

Types of Interview Questions

- **Theoretical Questions**
- Explain the virtual DOM in React.
- How does event delegation work in JavaScript?
- What are the differences between SQL and NoSQL databases?
- What are the advantages of using React Hooks over class components?
- Explain CORS and how to handle it in Express.js.
- How does MongoDB handle transactions?
- **Coding Challenges**
- Implement a function to debounce a React event handler.
- Write an Express.js middleware for error handling.
- Optimize MongoDB queries for performance.
- Implement an authentication system with JWT in MERN stack.

o   Write a function to paginate MongoDB query results.

o   Create a REST API endpoint to handle file uploads in Node.js.

o   **Debugging Tasks**

o   Identify and fix memory leaks in a Node.js application.

o   Debug a slow React component and improve rendering performance.

o   Fix a CORS error in an Express.js API.

o   Resolve a React state update issue in an asynchronous function.

o   Debug a failing unit test in a MERN project.

o   **System Design Questions**

o   Design a scalable e-commerce backend using MERN stack.

o   Architect a real-time chat application with WebSockets and MongoDB.

o   Design a job portal with React for frontend and Node.js backend.

o   Explain how you would optimize a high-traffic MERN application.

Example of a Typical Interview Question

● **Question:** *Design a URL shortener like Bit.ly using the MERN stack. What would your database schema look like, and how would you handle high traffic?*

How to Prepare Effectively for a MERN Stack Interview

Best Practices for Learning MERN Concepts Deeply

● **Master the Fundamentals**: Deep dive into JavaScript, ES6+ features, closures, promises, and async/await.

● **Understand Core React Concepts**: Hooks, Context API, performance optimization techniques (memoization, lazy loading).

● **Backend Best Practices**: Learn authentication

mechanisms, rate limiting, and API security.

Resources for Coding Challenges, Mock Interviews, and Projects

- **Coding Platforms**: LeetCode, HackerRank, CodeSignal (focus on DSA and JavaScript challenges).
- **Mock Interviews**: Participate in mock interviews on Pramp or Interviewing.io.
- **Hands-on Projects**: Build a **real-world application** (e.g., an e-commerce site, a task manager) and deploy it.

Importance of Hands-on Experience and Personal Projects

- **Build and Deploy**: Create full-stack projects, deploy on platforms like Vercel, Netlify, or AWS.
- **Contribute to Open Source**: Participate in GitHub projects, improving your portfolio and collaboration skills.
- **Engage with the Developer Community**: Join discussions on Stack Overflow, Medium, and Discord communities for MERN developers.

CHAPTER 2

MongoDB Essentials for Interviews

Introduction to MongoDB

What is MongoDB? Why is it Used in the MERN Stack?

- MongoDB is a **document-oriented NoSQL database** that stores data in a flexible, JSON-like format called BSON (Binary JSON). It is designed to handle large-scale data storage, high availability, and horizontal scalability. Unlike relational databases, MongoDB does not require a fixed schema, making it ideal for modern web applications that deal with dynamic and unstructured data.

- In the **MERN (MongoDB, Express.js, React, Node.js) stack**, MongoDB is the primary database used to store and retrieve application data. It integrates seamlessly with Node.js applications, providing a robust backend for web and mobile applications.

Key Differences Between SQL and NoSQL Databases

- **Feature**

  - **SQL Databases (Relational)**

    - **NoSQL Databases (MongoDB)**

- **Data Storage**

Uses tables with fixed schemas

Uses flexible, document-based storage

- **Scalability**

Scales vertically (adding resources to a single server)

Scales horizontally (adding more servers)

- **Schema**

Requires predefined schema

Schema-less and flexible

- **Joins**

Supports complex joins

Uses document references or embedding

- **Transactions**

Fully supports ACID transactions

Limited transaction support (introduced in MongoDB 4.0)

- **Best For**

Structured data with clear relationships

Unstructured, semi-structured, and rapidly changing data

Advantages and Disadvantages of Using MongoDB

- **Advantages:**
- **Flexibility:** No predefined schema allows easy modification of data structures.
- **Scalability:** Supports sharding for distributing data across multiple servers.
- **Performance:** Faster read/write operations compared to traditional relational databases.
- **JSON-Like Documents:** Native support for JavaScript (used in MERN stack).
- **High Availability:** Built-in replication ensures data redundancy.
- **Disadvantages:**
- **No Join Operations:** Complex relationships require manual data referencing.
- **Memory Usage:** Indexes and replication can consume significant memory.
- **ACID Limitations:** Transactions are not as robust as in SQL databases.

Core MongoDB Interview Questions and Answers

1. What is a Document in MongoDB? How Does It Differ from a Relational Database Table?

- A **document** in MongoDB is a BSON object that represents a record in a collection. It is similar to a row in a relational database but has a flexible structure.
- **Example of a MongoDB document:**

Json

Example:

```
{
  "_id": ObjectId("60c72b2f4f1a2564d9e5e123"),
  "name": "John Doe",
  "email": "john.doe@example.com",
  "age": 30,
  "address": {
    "city": "New York",
    "zip": "10001"
  }
}
```

- **Differences from Relational Tables:**
- No fixed schema: Fields can vary between documents in a collection.
- No predefined relationships: Embedding or referencing is used instead of joins.
- Faster reads and writes due to document-oriented storage.

2. Explain MongoDB Collections and How They Work

- A **collection** in MongoDB is equivalent to a table in relational databases but stores JSON-like documents instead of rows. Collections do not enforce a fixed schema, allowing flexible data storage.

javascript

Example:

```
db.users.insertOne({
  "name": "Alice",
  "email": "alice@example.com",
```

```
"role": "admin"
});
```

3. What Are the Key Data Types Supported in MongoDB?

MongoDB supports various data types, including:

- **String** – "name": "John Doe"
- **Number (Int, Double, Long, Decimal128)** – "age": 30
- **Boolean** – "isActive": true
- **Array** – "tags": ["developer", "blogger"]
- **Object** – Nested documents like "address": { "city": "New York" }
- **ObjectId** – Unique identifier for documents ("_id": ObjectId("..."))
- **Date** – Stores date and time values.

Schema Design Best Practices

1. How Do You Design an Efficient MongoDB Schema?

- Schema design should follow best practices to ensure **performance, scalability, and maintainability**:
- Store related data **together** using embedded documents for faster reads.
- Use **referencing** when data duplication needs to be minimized.
- Optimize for **query patterns** to reduce unnecessary reads and writes.
- Avoid **deeply nested structures** as they impact performance.

2. When Should You Embed vs. Reference Documents?

- **Scenario**

  - **Embed (Nested Document)**

- **Reference (Normalization)**

- **Data Read Frequency**

High

Low

- **Data Size**

Small

Large

- **Data Relationships**

One-to-few

One-to-many or many-to-many

- **Example**

User profile with address

User orders referencing products

Indexing and Performance Optimization

1. What Is an Index in MongoDB? How Does It Improve Performance?

- An **index** improves query performance by allowing MongoDB to quickly locate documents without scanning the entire collection.

Example: Creating an index on the email field:

javascript

Example:

```
db.users.createIndex({ "email": 1 });
```

2. How Do You Analyze and Optimize MongoDB Queries?

- Use **explain()** to analyze query execution:

javascript

Example:

```
db.users.find({                          "email":
"john@example.com" }).explain("executionStats");
```

Aggregation Framework

1. What Is the Aggregation Framework in MongoDB?

- MongoDB's **aggregation framework** processes data in a pipeline format to transform and analyze documents.

Example: Finding total sales by product category:

javascript

Example:

```
db.orders.aggregate([
  { $group: { _id: "$category", totalSales: { $sum: "$amount" } } }
]);
```

ACID vs BASE Properties in MongoDB

1. Does MongoDB Support ACID

Transactions? How Do They Work?

- MongoDB introduced **multi-document ACID transactions** in version 4.0, allowing atomic operations across multiple documents.

Example of a transaction:

```
const session = db.getMongo().startSession();

session.startTransaction();

try {

  db.accounts.updateOne({ "user": "Alice" }, { $inc: { "balance": -100 } });

  db.accounts.updateOne({ "user": "Bob" }, { $inc: { "balance": 100 } });

  session.commitTransaction();

} catch (e) {

  session.abortTransaction();

}

session.endSession();
```

Common MongoDB Commands and Queries

1. How to Insert, Update, Delete, and Query Documents?

- **Insert:** db.users.insertOne({ "name": "Alice" })
- **Update:** db.users.updateOne({ "name": "Alice" }, { $set: { "age": 25 } })
- **Delete:** db.users.deleteOne({ "name": "Alice" })
- **Query:** db.users.find({ "age": { $gt: 20 } })

Expert Tips for MongoDB Interviews

- **Understand real-world use cases** and how MongoDB is used in production.
- **Practice system design** questions related to MongoDB architecture.
- **Use indexes effectively** to optimize performance.
- **Avoid excessive embedding** to prevent large document sizes.
- **Familiarize yourself with the aggregation framework** for data transformation.

CHAPTER 3

Advanced MongoDB Concepts

1. Introduction to Advanced MongoDB Concepts

- As companies scale their applications to handle millions of users and vast amounts of data, advanced MongoDB concepts become crucial for ensuring **high availability, performance, and data integrity**. In MNC technical interviews, candidates are often tested on their **ability to design scalable architectures, optimize queries, and implement fault-tolerant solutions** using MongoDB.

Real-World Use Cases of Advanced MongoDB Concepts

- **E-commerce Platforms:** Large-scale applications like Amazon and Flipkart require replication and sharding to handle millions of product listings and user transactions.
- **Financial Systems:** Banking applications need **ACID transactions** for ensuring atomicity in money transfers.
- **Real-Time Analytics:** Social media and streaming platforms use **aggregation pipelines** for insights into user engagement.
- **IoT Applications:** High-throughput data ingestion from IoT devices requires optimized indexing strategies.

Challenges Faced in Large-Scale MongoDB Deployments

- **Replication Delays** – Data synchronization issues in replica sets.
- **Shard Key Selection** – Choosing an optimal shard key to

avoid uneven data distribution.
- **Query Performance Bottlenecks** – Inefficient indexing and slow queries.
- **High Availability & Disaster Recovery** – Ensuring database resilience against failures.

---

2. Replication in MongoDB

What is Replication and Why is it Needed?

- Replication in MongoDB is used to **maintain multiple copies of data** across different servers to ensure high availability and fault tolerance. It protects against hardware failures and enables distributed read operations.

Understanding Replica Sets in MongoDB

- A **replica set** consists of:
- **Primary Node** – Handles write operations.
- **Secondary Nodes** – Maintain copies of the data and serve read operations.
- **Arbiter Node** (Optional) – Participates in elections but does not store data.

Step-by-Step Guide to Setting Up a Replica Set

Start multiple MongoDB instances:
bash
Example:

```
mongod --replSet "rs0" --port 27017 --dbpath /data/db1

mongod --replSet "rs0" --port 27018 --dbpath /data/db2

mongod --replSet "rs0" --port 27019 --dbpath /data/db3
```

1. **Connect to MongoDB and initiate the replica set:**
   Example:
   rs.initiate({

```
_id: "rs0",
```

```
members: [

  { _id: 0, host: "localhost:27017" },

  { _id: 1, host: "localhost:27018" },

  { _id: 2, host: "localhost:27019" }

]

});
```

2. Common Replication Issues and Troubleshooting

- **Replication Lag** – Check secondary nodes using rs.status() and adjust write concern.
- **Elections & Failover Delays** – Optimize heartbeat settings and priority configurations.

Interview Question: How Does MongoDB Handle Failover in a Replica Set?

- **Answer:** When the primary node fails, an election is triggered among the secondary nodes. The node with the highest priority becomes the new primary. The arbiter (if present) helps in breaking ties but does not store data.

3. Sharding in MongoDB

What is Sharding and When Should It Be Used?

- Sharding **distributes large datasets across multiple servers** to ensure scalability and load balancing. It is used when a single server cannot handle all the data efficiently.

Key Components of Sharding

- **Shard Key** – Determines how data is distributed.
- **Config Servers** – Store metadata and manage cluster state.
- **Mongos Router** – Routes client requests to the appropriate shard.

Steps to Implement Sharding in Production

Enable sharding:
Example:
```
sh.enableSharding("myDatabase");
```

Choose a shard key and create an index:
Example:
```
db.myCollection.createIndex({ userId: 1 });

sh.shardCollection("myDatabase.myCollection", { userId: 1 });
```

Interview Question: How Do You Choose the Right Shard Key?

- **Answer:** The shard key should distribute data **evenly** to prevent hotspots. Consider:
- **High cardinality** (e.g., userId instead of country).
- **Balanced read/write load** across shards.
- **Query patterns** to avoid frequent cross-shard queries.

4. Transactions in MongoDB

What are ACID Transactions in MongoDB?

- MongoDB supports **multi-document ACID transactions**, ensuring:
- **Atomicity** – All operations succeed or none are applied.
- **Consistency** – Data integrity is maintained.
- **Isolation** – Transactions do not interfere with each other.
- **Durability** – Committed transactions persist.

Performing Multi-Document Transactions

Example:
```
const session = db.getMongo().startSession();

session.startTransaction();

try {
```

```
db.users.updateOne({ _id: 1 }, { $set: { balance: 500 } },
{ session });

db.transactions.insertOne({ userId: 1, amount: -500 },
{ session });

session.commitTransaction();
} catch (e) {

session.abortTransaction();

}

session.endSession();
```

Interview Question: When Would You Use Transactions Over Single-Document Operations?

- **Answer:** When multiple collections or documents need to be updated together, such as **bank transactions** or **inventory management**.

5. MongoDB Indexing Strategies

Types of Indexes

- **Single Field Index:** db.collection.createIndex({ email: 1 })
- **Compound Index:** db.collection.createIndex({ firstName: 1, lastName: 1 })
- **Multikey Index:** Supports array fields.
- **Text Index:** Full-text search capabilities.
- **Geospatial Index:** Location-based queries.

Interview Question: How Would You Optimize a Slow Query?

- **Answer:** Use explain("executionStats") to analyze query performance and optimize indexing.

6. Aggregation Framework

Aggregation Pipeline Stages

- $match – Filters documents.
- $group – Groups documents.
- $project – Shapes output.
- $sort – Orders results.
- $limit – Restricts output count.

Example: Aggregating Sales Data

Example:

db.sales.aggregate([

  { $match: { status: "completed" } },

  { $group: { _id: "$category", totalRevenue: { $sum: "$amount" } } },

  { $sort: { totalRevenue: -1 } }

]);

7. Performance Optimization Techniques

- **Use Projections:** Return only necessary fields.
- **Optimize Index Usage:** Avoid redundant indexes.
- **Partition Large Datasets:** Use **sharding** effectively.
- **Monitor Performance:** Use MongoDB Profiler.

8. Backup and Disaster Recovery Strategies

- **Mongodump & Mongorestore:** Basic backup strategy.
- **Oplog Backup:** Continuous replication for recovery.
- **Automated Snapshots:** Cloud-based backups.

9. Common MongoDB Interview Scenarios

- **Scenario:** How to handle a **multi-region deployment** with MongoDB?
  Solution: Use **replica sets across regions**, with nearest read preference.
- **Scenario:** Optimizing a **high-traffic API backend.**
  Solution: Use **sharding, caching (Redis), and connection pooling.**

10. Conclusion and Key Takeaways

- **Master replication and sharding** for **scalability and availability.**
- **Use indexing effectively** to **optimize query performance.**
- **Leverage aggregation** for **complex data processing.**
- **Understand ACID transactions** for **data integrity.**
- **Recommended Resources:**
- MongoDB University
- "MongoDB in Action" by Kyle Banker
- Official MongoDB Documentation

CHAPTER 4

Express.js Fundamentals

1. Introduction to Express.js

What is Express.js, and Why is It Used in Web Development?

- Express.js is a **minimalist, unopinionated web application framework for Node.js** that simplifies building server-side applications. It provides a robust set of features for creating APIs, handling HTTP requests, and managing middleware efficiently.

In raw Node.js, developers must manually handle routing, request parsing, and response management, making development cumbersome. Express.js abstracts these complexities, allowing developers to focus on business logic instead of low-level server configurations.

Key Features of Express.js

- **Middleware Support** – Allows adding custom logic for request processing.
- **Routing System** – Supports **dynamic and modular routing**.
- **Template Engine Support** – Works with **EJS, Pug, and Handlebars** for rendering dynamic views.
- **Error Handling** – Provides built-in mechanisms for handling **synchronous and asynchronous errors**.
- **Security & Performance** – Supports security measures like

CORS, rate limiting, and Helmet.js.
- **Database Integration** – Easily connects with MongoDB using **Mongoose**.

Real-World Applications of Express.js

- **RESTful APIs** – Used by companies like Uber and Airbnb to build API-driven applications.
- **Server-Side Rendering (SSR)** – E-commerce platforms render pages dynamically for SEO benefits.
- **Real-Time Applications** – Chat applications and collaborative tools using WebSockets.
- **Microservices** – Large-scale applications breaking down functionality into independent services.

2. Setting Up an Express.js Application

Installing Express.js Using npm

To install Express.js in a Node.js project, run:

Example:

```
mkdir express-app && cd express-app

npm init -y

npm install express
```

Creating a Basic Express.js Server

Example:

```
const express = require('express');

const app = express();

app.get('/', (req, res) => {

    res.send('Hello, Express!');

});
```

```
app.listen(3000, () => {
    console.log('Server running on http://localhost:3000');
});
```

Understanding app.listen() and Handling Requests

- app.listen(port, callback) starts the server.
- The callback function executes when the server starts.

3. Understanding Express.js Routing

What is Routing in Express.js?

- Routing determines how an application **handles HTTP requests**.

Creating Routes Using HTTP Methods

Example:

```
app.get('/users', (req, res) => res.send('GET Users'));

app.post('/users', (req, res) => res.send('POST User'));

app.put('/users/:id', (req, res) => res.send(`Update User ${req.params.id}`));

app.delete('/users/:id', (req, res) => res.send(`Delete User ${req.params.id}`));
```

Route Parameters and Query Strings

Example:

```
app.get('/products/:id', (req, res) => {
    res.send(`Product ID: ${req.params.id}`);
```

```
});


app.get('/search', (req, res) => {
    res.send(`Search Query: ${req.query.q}`);
});
```

Using express.Router() for Modular Routing

Example:

```
const router = express.Router();
router.get('/', (req, res) => res.send('All Users'));
router.post('/', (req, res) => res.send('Add User'));


app.use('/users', router);
```

---

4. Middleware in Express.js

What is Middleware?

- Middleware functions execute **before the request reaches the route handler**.

Types of Middleware in Express.js

- **Built-in Middleware:** express.json(), express.static().
- **Third-Party Middleware:** morgan (logging), helmet (security).
- **Custom Middleware:** Logging, authentication, validation.

Implementing Middleware for Logging

Example:

```
const logger = (req, res, next) => {
    console.log(` ${req.method} ${req.url}`);
    next();
};


app.use(logger);
```

---

5. Handling Requests and Responses

Understanding req and res Objects

- req – Contains HTTP request details.
- res – Used to send responses.

Sending JSON Responses

javascript

Example:

```
app.get('/json', (req, res) => {
    res.json({ message: 'Hello, JSON' });
});
```

Handling Redirects and File Downloads

Example:

```
app.get('/redirect', (req, res) => res.redirect('/json'));
app.get('/download', (req, res) => res.download('file.pdf'));
```

---

6. Express.js with Template Engines

Rendering Dynamic Content Using EJS

bash

Example:

npm install ejs

javascript

Example:

```
app.set('view engine', 'ejs');

app.get('/welcome', (req, res) => {
    res.render('welcome', { name: 'John' });
});
```

EJS Template (views/welcome.ejs)

html

Example:

```
<h1>Welcome, <%= name %>!</h1>
```

7. Error Handling in Express.js

Creating Custom Error-Handling Middleware

Example:

```
app.use((err, req, res, next) => {
    console.error(err.stack);
    res.status(500).send('Something broke!');
```

```
});
```

---

8. Working with Static Files in Express.js

Serving Static Files

Example:

```
app.use(express.static('public'));
```

- Store **CSS, JavaScript, images** in the public directory.

---

9. Connecting Express.js with MongoDB

Installing and Configuring Mongoose

bash

Example:

```
npm install mongoose
```

javascript

Example:

```
const mongoose = require('mongoose');
mongoose.connect('mongodb://localhost:27017/mydb');
```

Creating a REST API with Express.js and MongoDB

javascript

Example:

```
const User = mongoose.model('User', { name: String });
```

```
app.post('/users', async (req, res) => {
    const user = new User({ name: req.body.name });
    await user.save();
    res.send(user);
});
```

10. Security Best Practices in Express.js

Preventing Common Vulnerabilities

- **Helmet.js for Security Headers:**
  javascript
  Example:
  const helmet = require('helmet');

```
app.use(helmet());
```

- **CORS Handling:**
  javascript
  Example:
  const cors = require('cors');

```
app.use(cors());
```

11. Performance Optimization in Express.js

Optimizing Middleware Execution

- Place frequently used middleware **before route handlers** for better performance.

Using Clustering for High Traffic

javascript

Example:

```
const cluster = require('cluster');

const os = require('os');


if (cluster.isMaster) {

    os.cpus().forEach(() => cluster.fork());

} else {

    app.listen(3000);

}
```

12. Conclusion and Key Takeaways

- **Express.js simplifies backend development** with middleware, routing, and API support.
- **Use modular routing with** express.Router() to improve maintainability.
- **Middleware functions** play a crucial role in authentication, logging, and error handling.
- **Security best practices** like Helmet.js and CORS prevent vulnerabilities.

Common Interview Questions

- **How does Express.js differ from Node.js's built-in HTTP module?**
  Answer: Express.js provides built-in routing, middleware support, and request parsing, reducing manual effort compared to raw Node.js.

- **How do you handle errors in Express.js?**
  Answer: Use a custom error-handling middleware function with four parameters (err, req, res, next).

- **What is the purpose of** express.Router()?
  Answer: It enables modular routing, separating route logic into different files for better organization.

CHAPTER 5

Authentication and Security in Express.js

1. Introduction to Authentication and Security in Express.js

Overview of Authentication and Authorization

- Authentication and security are fundamental to modern web applications. **Authentication** verifies the identity of users, while **authorization** determines what actions they can perform within an application. In **Express.js**, authentication is crucial for protecting API endpoints, preventing unauthorized access, and ensuring secure data transactions.

Why Security is Critical in Modern Web Applications

- **Data Protection** – Prevents unauthorized access to sensitive user data.
- **Compliance** – Meets industry security standards like **OAuth, GDPR, and HIPAA**.
- **User Trust** – Ensures a secure environment for transactions and user interactions.
- **Prevention of Attacks** – Guards against common vulnerabilities like **SQL Injection, XSS, and CSRF**.

Common Security Threats in Express.js Applications

- **Brute-force attacks** – Automated attempts to guess passwords.
- **Cross-Site Scripting (XSS)** – Injecting malicious scripts into web pages.
- **Cross-Site Request Forgery (CSRF)** – Exploiting authenticated user sessions.
- **Man-in-the-Middle (MITM) Attacks** – Intercepting unencrypted HTTP requests.

2. Understanding Authentication Methods

Session-Based Authentication (Express Sessions)

- Session-based authentication stores user credentials on the server. It uses **cookies** to maintain authentication.
- **Implementation:**

javascript

Example:

```
const express = require('express');
const session = require('express-session');

const app = express();
app.use(session({
  secret: 'secureRandomString',
  resave: false,
  saveUninitialized: true,
  cookie: { secure: false }
}));

app.get('/', (req, res) => {
```

```
req.session.user = "JohnDoe";

res.send('Session set!');

});
```

- **Drawbacks:**
- Not scalable for distributed systems.
- Requires session management on the server.

Token-Based Authentication (JWT - JSON Web Token)

- JWT authentication is **stateless** and is widely used in REST APIs. A JWT contains a **payload**, **header**, and **signature**, which verifies authenticity.

OAuth 2.0 Authentication and Social Logins

- OAuth allows third-party authentication via services like **Google, GitHub, and Facebook.**
- **Example OAuth Flow:**
  1. User clicks "Login with Google."
  2. Redirected to Google's authorization server.
  3. User grants permissions.
  4. Google issues an access token.
  5. The application uses this token to authenticate API requests.

API Key Authentication

API keys authenticate machine-to-machine communication. It is used in:

- Third-party API consumption.
- Internal service authentication.

3. Implementing JWT Authentication in Express.js

How JWT Works in Authentication

- User logs in with credentials.
- Server validates credentials and generates a JWT.
- JWT is stored in **localStorage/cookies**.
- Each request includes JWT in the Authorization header.
- The server verifies and allows/denies access.

Setting Up JWT Authentication with Express.js and MongoDB

- **Install Dependencies**

bash

Example:

```
npm install express jsonwebtoken bcryptjs mongoose dotenv
```

- **User Authentication and Token Signing**

javascript

Example:

```javascript
const express = require('express');

const jwt = require('jsonwebtoken');

const bcrypt = require('bcryptjs');

const User = require('./models/User');

const app = express();

app.use(express.json());


app.post('/login', async (req, res) => {
  const user = await User.findOne({ email: req.body.email });
  if (!user || !await bcrypt.compare(req.body.password,
user.password)) {
    return res.status(401).json({ error: "Invalid credentials" });
```

```
}
```

```
const token = jwt.sign({ id: user._id },
process.env.JWT_SECRET, { expiresIn: '1h' });
  res.json({ token });
});
```

Verifying JWT and Protecting Routes

javascript

Example:

```
const authenticateJWT = (req, res, next) => {
  const token = req.header('Authorization');
  if (!token) return res.status(401).send('Access Denied');

  jwt.verify(token, process.env.JWT_SECRET, (err, user) => {
    if (err) return res.status(403).send('Invalid Token');
    req.user = user;
    next();
  });
};

app.get('/dashboard', authenticateJWT, (req, res) => {
  res.json({ message: "Welcome to the dashboard!" });
});
```

4. Implementing OAuth 2.0 and Social Login

Using Passport.js for OAuth Authentication

- **Installing Passport.js and Google Strategy**

bash

Example:

```
npm install passport passport-google-oauth20 express-session
```

- **Configuring Google Authentication**

javascript

Example:

```javascript
const passport = require('passport');
const GoogleStrategy = require('passport-google-oauth20').Strategy;

passport.use(new GoogleStrategy({
  clientID: process.env.GOOGLE_CLIENT_ID,
  clientSecret: process.env.GOOGLE_CLIENT_SECRET,
  callbackURL: "/auth/google/callback"
}, (accessToken, refreshToken, profile, done) => {
  return done(null, profile);
}));

app.get('/auth/google', passport.authenticate('google', { scope: ['profile', 'email'] }));
```

```javascript
app.get('/auth/google/callback', passport.authenticate('google',
{ failureRedirect: '/' }), (req, res) => {
  res.redirect('/dashboard');
});
```

---

5. Role-Based Access Control (RBAC) in Express.js

Implementing Role-Based Authentication with Middleware

javascript

Example:

```javascript
const checkRole = (role) => (req, res, next) => {
  if (req.user.role !== role) {
    return res.status(403).json({ error: "Access Denied" });
  }
  next();
};


app.get('/admin', authenticateJWT, checkRole('admin'), (req, res)
=> {
  res.send('Admin Panel');
});
```

---

6. Common Security Vulnerabilities and Prevention

Preventing SQL & NoSQL Injection

Use parameterized queries in MongoDB:

javascript

Example:

```
User.findOne({ email: req.body.email }); // Prevents NoSQL injection
```

Mitigating XSS Attacks

- Sanitize input with libraries like **express-validator**.
- Use **Content Security Policy (CSP)** headers.

CSRF Protection Techniques

- Use **CSRF tokens** with csurf middleware.
- Enforce **same-site cookies** for sensitive requests.

Using Helmet.js for Secure Headers

javascript

Example:

```
const helmet = require('helmet');

app.use(helmet());
```

7. Secure Authentication Best Practices

Storing Passwords Securely with Bcrypt

javascript

Example:

```
const hashedPassword = await bcrypt.hash(req.body.password, 10);
```

Implementing Rate Limiting to Prevent Brute-Force Attacks

javascript

Example:

```
const rateLimit = require('express-rate-limit');
app.use(rateLimit({ windowMs: 15 * 60 * 1000, max: 100 }));
```

Using HTTPS and Secure Cookies

- Enable HTTPS in production.
- Set **Secure and HttpOnly** flags for cookies.

8. Real-World Interview Questions and Answers

1. How do you protect an Express.js API against XSS attacks?

Answer: Use **input validation, escaping HTML characters, and Content Security Policy (CSP) headers.

2. How would you handle authentication in a microservices architecture?

- *Answer:* Use **OAuth 2.0** or **JWT-based authentication** with a central authentication server.

3. What are the best practices for securing API endpoints in Express.js?

Answer:

- Implement **JWT authentication**.
- Use **rate limiting** to prevent abuse.
- Enable **CORS** with proper configurations.
- Implement **role-based access control (RBAC)**.

Authentication and security are critical aspects of modern Express.js applications. This chapter covered:

- **Authentication methods** (Sessions, JWT, OAuth, API Keys).
- **Role-Based Access Control (RBAC)** for secure authorization.
- **Preventing vulnerabilities** like **XSS, CSRF, and SQL injection**.
- **Best practices** for securing Express.js applications.

CHAPTER 6

Node.js Essentials for Interviews

1. Introduction to Node.js

Overview of Node.js and Its Importance in Modern Web Development

- Node.js is a **runtime environment** that allows developers to execute JavaScript code outside the browser, using Google's **V8 JavaScript engine**. It is widely used for **server-side programming**, making JavaScript a full-stack language.
- **Why is Node.js Important?**
- **Non-blocking, event-driven architecture** – Enables efficient handling of multiple concurrent requests.
- **Single programming language (JavaScript)** – Used across frontend and backend.
- **High performance** – Powered by the V8 engine, optimized for fast execution.
- **Large ecosystem** – npm provides access to thousands of packages.

Key Features and Benefits of Node.js

- **Asynchronous & Non-Blocking I/O** – Ensures fast and scalable applications.
- **Event-Driven Architecture** – Efficiently handles multiple

requests.

- **Scalability** – Built-in support for clustering and load balancing.
- **Lightweight & Fast Execution** – Uses a single-threaded model.

Common Use Cases of Node.js in Real-World Applications

- **REST APIs & Microservices** – Used by companies like Netflix and PayPal.
- **Real-Time Applications** – Chat apps, gaming platforms (e.g., WebSockets).
- **Streaming Services** – YouTube, Twitch use Node.js for video processing.
- **IoT Applications** – Handles millions of device connections efficiently.

2. Asynchronous Programming in Node.js

Synchronous vs. Asynchronous Programming

Feature	Synchronous	Asynchronous
Execution	One task at a time	Multiple tasks simultaneously
Performance	Slower	Faster
Blocking	Blocks the thread	Non-blocking

Event-Driven Architecture in Node.js

- Node.js relies on an **event-driven model**, where it listens for events and executes callbacks when an event occurs.
- **Example: Event Listener in Node.js**

javascript

Example:

```
const EventEmitter = require('events');
const eventEmitter = new EventEmitter();


eventEmitter.on('greet', (name) => {
    console.log(`Hello, ${name}!`);
});


eventEmitter.emit('greet', 'Alice');
```

Callbacks in Node.js

- A **callback function** is a function passed as an argument to another function and executed later.

javascript

Example:

```
function fetchData(callback) {
    setTimeout(() => {
        callback('Data fetched');
    }, 2000);
}


fetchData((message) => {
    console.log(message);
});
```

Callback Hell and How to Avoid It

- Nested callbacks lead to **callback hell,** making code difficult to read and maintain.
- **Example of Callback Hell**

javascript

Example:

```
fs.readFile('file1.txt', (err, data1) => {
    fs.readFile('file2.txt', (err, data2) => {
        fs.readFile('file3.txt', (err, data3) => {
            console.log(data1, data2, data3);
        });
    });
});
```

- **Solution: Using Promises or Async/Await**

javascript

Example:

```
const fs = require('fs').promises;

async function readFiles() {
    const data1 = await fs.readFile('file1.txt');
    const data2 = await fs.readFile('file2.txt');
    const data3 = await fs.readFile('file3.txt');
    console.log(data1, data2, data3);
}
readFiles();
```

3. Promises and Async/Await in Node.js

Introduction to Promises

- A **Promise** represents a future value that may resolve or reject.

javascript

Example:

```javascript
const fetchData = new Promise((resolve, reject) => {
    setTimeout(() => resolve("Data loaded"), 2000);
});


fetchData.then(data => console.log(data)).catch(err => console.log(err));
```

Chaining Promises and Handling Errors

javascript

Example:

```javascript
fetchData
  .then(data => {
    console.log(data);
    return "Next step";
  })
  .then(step => console.log(step))
  .catch(error => console.error(error));
```

Understanding Async/Await

async/await simplifies handling asynchronous operations.

javascript

Example:

```
async function fetchData() {
    try {
        const data = await fetchDataFromDB();
        console.log(data);
    } catch (error) {
        console.error(error);
    }
}
```

4. The Event Loop in Node.js

How the Event Loop Works

- The **event loop** manages asynchronous operations, ensuring Node.js remains non-blocking.

Phases of the Event Loop

- **Timers** – Executes setTimeout and setInterval.
- **I/O Callbacks** – Handles asynchronous I/O.
- **Idle & Prepare** – Internal processing.
- **Poll** – Retrieves new I/O events.
- **Check** – Executes setImmediate callbacks.
- **Close Callbacks** – Executes socket.on('close').

5. Streams and Buffers in Node.js

Types of Streams

- **Readable Streams** – Read data (e.g., fs.createReadStream).
- **Writable Streams** – Write data.
- **Duplex Streams** – Read and write (e.g., TCP sockets).
- **Transform Streams** – Modify data (e.g., gzip compression).
- **Example: Reading a File Using Streams**

javascript

Example:

```javascript
const fs = require('fs');

const readStream = fs.createReadStream('file.txt');

readStream.on('data', chunk => console.log(chunk.toString()));
```

---

6. Process Management in Node.js

Using Child Processes

javascript

Example:

```javascript
const { exec } = require('child_process');
exec('ls', (error, stdout) => console.log(stdout));
```

Using Clustering for Load Balancing

javascript

Example:

```javascript
const cluster = require('cluster');
const http = require('http');
```

```
const os = require('os');


if (cluster.isMaster) {

    os.cpus().forEach(() => cluster.fork());

} else {

    http.createServer((req,      res)      =>      res.end('Hello
World')).listen(8000);

}
```

7. Error Handling in Node.js

Handling Synchronous Errors

javascript

Example:

```
try {

    throw new Error("Something went wrong");

} catch (error) {

    console.error(error);

}
```

Handling Asynchronous Errors

javascript

Example:

```
process.on('unhandledRejection', (reason, promise) => {

    console.error('Unhandled rejection:', reason);
```

```
});
```

8. Node.js Performance Optimization Techniques

Best Practices for Memory Management

- Use **streams** instead of loading entire files into memory.
- Optimize **database queries**.
- Use **garbage collection monitoring**.

Caching for Performance Improvement

javascript

Example:

```
const cache = {};
function getCachedData(key) {
    if (cache[key]) return cache[key];
    cache[key] = expensiveFunction();
    return cache[key];
}
```

9. Common Node.js Interview Questions and Answers

1. What is the difference between process.nextTick() and setImmediate()?

- process.nextTick() executes **before** the next event loop phase.
- setImmediate() executes **after** the I/O phase.

2. How does Node.js handle concurrent requests with a single-threaded model?

- It uses **event-driven, non-blocking I/O** via the **event loop**.

3. How do you prevent memory leaks in a Node.js application?

- Use **event listener cleanup** (removeListener).
- Avoid **global variables**.
- Profile memory usage with **heap snapshots**.

10. Summary and Key Takeaways

- **Node.js is asynchronous and event-driven**, making it highly efficient for web applications.
- **Promises and async/await** help manage asynchronous code effectively.
- **The event loop handles I/O operations efficiently**, preventing blocking.
- **Performance optimization** can be achieved with **caching, clustering, and memory management**.

Further Learning Resources

- **Official Node.js Documentation**
- **"Node.js Design Patterns" by Mario Casciaro**
- **"Mastering Node.js" by Sandro Pasquali**

CHAPTER 7

Advanced Node.js Concepts

1. Optimizing Node.js Performance

Performance optimization is critical when working with Node.js, especially for large-scale applications handling millions of requests per day. This section explores how to identify bottlenecks and improve the efficiency of Node.js applications.

How to Profile and Optimize a Node.js Application

- **Using the Node.js Built-in Profiler**

The built-in --prof flag generates a log file for CPU profiling:

bash

Example:

```
node --prof app.js
node --prof-process isolate-*.log
```

- **Using Chrome DevTools for Profiling**

Start your Node.js application with:
bash
Example:
```
node --inspect app.js
```

Open Chrome and navigate to chrome://inspect.

- Use the **Profiler** to analyze memory and CPU usage.

Identifying Performance Bottlenecks

Common bottlenecks include:

- **Blocking operations** (e.g., large synchronous computations).
- **Excessive garbage collection** causing memory leaks.
- **Slow database queries** due to missing indexes.

Techniques for Reducing Memory Leaks

- **Avoid global variables** that persist beyond their required scope.
- **Use WeakMap for caching** to allow automatic garbage collection.
- **Monitor memory usage** using the process.memoryUsage() function.

Using Performance Monitoring Tools

- **PM2:** Process manager for running and monitoring applications.
  bash
  Example:
  pm2 start app.js --watch

pm2 monit

- **New Relic:** Tracks real-time performance metrics in production.

2. Handling Large-Scale Applications in Node.js

Best Practices for Enterprise-Level Applications

- Use **modular architecture** (separate routes, controllers, services).

- Implement **middleware caching** (Redis, Memcached).
- Design with **horizontal scalability** in mind (clustering, load balancing).

Managing High Concurrency with Event-Driven Architecture

- Node.js' event-driven model efficiently handles thousands of concurrent connections using **non-blocking I/O**.

javascript

Example:

```
const http = require('http');
http.createServer((req, res) => {
    res.end('Hello, World!');
}).listen(3000);
```

Distributed Systems and Microservices in Node.js

- **Netflix & PayPal** use Node.js to manage microservices at scale.
- Use **Docker & Kubernetes** for deploying scalable services.
- Implement **message queues (RabbitMQ, Kafka)** for inter-service communication.

3. Load Balancing and Clustering in Node.js

Understanding Single-Threaded vs Multi-Threaded Architectures

- Node.js runs on a **single thread**, but we can utilize **clustering** to take advantage of multi-core processors.

Implementing the Cluster Module in Node.js

javascript

Example:
```
const cluster = require('cluster');
const os = require('os');

if (cluster.isMaster) {
    os.cpus().forEach(() => cluster.fork());
} else {
    require('./server'); // Worker process
}
```

Using Nginx as a Reverse Proxy

Install Nginx:
bash
Example:
```
sudo apt install nginx
```

Configure /etc/nginx/sites-available/default:
nginx
Example:
```
upstream nodeapp {
    server 127.0.0.1:3000;
    server 127.0.0.1:3001;
}

server {
    listen 80;
    location / {
        proxy_pass http://nodeapp;
```

```
    }
}
```

4. Advanced Asynchronous Processing

Deep Dive into the Event Loop

- **Microtasks (Promises,** process.nextTick**)** execute before the next event loop phase.
- **Macrotasks (**setTimeout, setImmediate**)** execute after the current phase.

Using Worker Threads for CPU-Intensive Tasks

javascript

Example:

```javascript
const { Worker } = require('worker_threads');
const worker = new Worker('./worker.js');


worker.on('message', message => console.log(message));
worker.postMessage({ task: 'heavy-computation' });
```

5. WebSockets and Real-Time Communication

Implementing a Real-Time Chat App Using WebSockets

Install ws:

bash

Example:

```bash
npm install ws
```

Server-side implementation:

javascript

Example:

```
const WebSocket = require('ws');
const server = new WebSocket.Server({ port: 8080 });


server.on('connection', ws => {
    ws.on('message', message => console.log(`Received: $
{message}`));
    ws.send('Welcome to WebSocket Server!');
});
```

6. Secure Coding Practices in Node.js

Common Security Vulnerabilities

- **SQL Injection** – Use parameterized queries with **Mongoose**:
  javascript
  Example:
  ```
  User.findOne({ email: req.body.email }); // Prevents
  injection
  ```
- **Cross-Site Scripting (XSS)** – Sanitize input with express-validator.
- **Cross-Site Request Forgery (CSRF)** – Use csurf middleware.

Securing APIs with Authentication & Authorization

- Use **JWT** for stateless authentication.
- Implement **OAuth2** for third-party authentication.
- Restrict access with **Role-Based Access Control (RBAC)**.

7. Caching Strategies for Node.js Applications

Improving Performance with Redis

Install Redis:

bash

Example:

npm install redis

Cache API responses:

javascript

Example:

```
const redis = require('redis');
const client = redis.createClient();

app.get('/data', async (req, res) => {
    const cache = await client.get('data');
    if (cache) return res.json(JSON.parse(cache));

    const freshData = await fetchData();
    client.setex('data', 3600, JSON.stringify(freshData));
    res.json(freshData);
});
```

8. Implementing Microservices Architecture in Node.js

Breaking a Monolith into Microservices

- **Each microservice has its own database** for data autonomy.
- **Use REST or gRPC** for inter-service communication.

Using Docker and Kubernetes for Deployment

Dockerfile:

dockerfile

Example:

```
FROM node:14
WORKDIR /app
COPY . .
RUN npm install
CMD ["node", "server.js"]
```

Deploying with Kubernetes:

yaml

Example:

```
apiVersion: apps/v1
kind: Deployment
metadata:
  name: node-app
spec:
  replicas: 3
  template:
    spec:
      containers:
      - name: node-app
```

image: mynodeapp

---

9. Error Handling and Debugging

Using Winston for Logging

javascript

Example:

```javascript
const winston = require('winston');
const logger = winston.createLogger({
    level: 'info',
    transports: [
        new winston.transports.File({ filename: 'error.log' })
    ]
});
```

Handling Uncaught Exceptions and Promises

javascript

Example:

```javascript
process.on('uncaughtException', err => {
    console.error('Uncaught Exception:', err);
});

process.on('unhandledRejection', err => {
    console.error('Unhandled Rejection:', err);
});
```

10. Real-World MNC-Level Interview Questions on Advanced Node.js

Scenario-Based Questions

- **How would you handle 10,000 concurrent WebSocket connections in Node.js?**
  Answer: Use **WebSocket clustering with Redis Pub/Sub** for message distribution.

- **How do you prevent memory leaks in a long-running Node.js application?**
  Answer: Use **profiling tools, garbage collection tuning**, and **event listener cleanup**.

- **How do you design a scalable Node.js microservice for an e-commerce platform?**
  Answer: Implement **service discovery, API gateways, and RabbitMQ for event-driven communication**.

This chapter covered:

- **Performance optimization, caching, and security best practices.**
- **Advanced asynchronous processing with Worker Threads.**
- **Microservices architecture and real-time applications with WebSockets.**
- **Scalable architecture patterns for enterprise applications.**

CHAPTER 8

React.js Basics for Interviews

1. Introduction to React.js

Brief History and Evolution of React.js

- React.js was developed by **Jordan Walke** at **Facebook** in **2011** to address performance and maintainability issues in Facebook's UI. It was open-sourced in **2013** and has since become one of the most popular frontend libraries for building user interfaces.

Why React.js is Widely Used in Modern Web Development

- **Component-Based Architecture** – Encourages reusable, modular UI components.
- **Virtual DOM** – Efficiently updates only the necessary parts of the UI.
- **Declarative UI** – Simplifies complex UI logic with a predictable state.
- **Strong Community & Ecosystem** – Backed by Facebook and a large open-source community.

Comparison with Other Frontend Frameworks

Feature	React.js	Angular	Vue.js
Type	Library	Framework	Framework
Language	JavaScript, JSX	TypeScript	JavaScript

• **Architecture**	Component-Based	MVC	Component-Based
• **DOM Handling**	Virtual DOM	Real DOM	Virtual DOM
• **State Management**	Built-in (useState, Context API)	RxJS, NgRx	Vuex, Pinia

2. React.js Interview Questions on Components

What are React Components? Explain Functional vs. Class Components.

- Components are **building blocks of a React application**. They can be **functional** or **class-based**.
- **Functional Component Example:**

javascript

Example:

```
const Greeting = ({ name }) => <h1>Hello, {name}!</h1>;
export default Greeting;
```

- **Class Component Example:**

javascript

Example:

```
import React, { Component } from 'react';

class Greeting extends Component {
  render() {
    return <h1>Hello, {this.props.name}!</h1>;
  }
}
```

export default Greeting;

- **Key Differences:**
- **Functional components** are stateless but can use **React Hooks**.
- **Class components** have **state** and lifecycle methods.

When to Use Functional Components Instead of Class Components?

- Functional components are **preferred** due to better performance and simpler syntax.
- Use **functional components** with **hooks** for managing state and side effects.

How Do Props Work in React? Provide Examples.

- Props (**properties**) allow **data flow from parent to child components**.

javascript

Example:

const UserProfile = ({ name, age }) => <p>{name} is {age} years old.</p>;

<UserProfile name="Alice" age={25} />;

- **Props are Read-Only:** They **cannot be modified** inside the child component.

3. React Lifecycle Methods (For Class Components)

Explain the Lifecycle Phases of a React Component

- React components go through **three main phases**:
- **Mounting** – Component is created (componentDidMount).
- **Updating** – Component updates on state/prop changes (componentDidUpdate).
- **Unmounting** – Component is removed (componentWillUnmount).

What is the Purpose of componentDidMount, componentDidUpdate, and componentWillUnmount?

Lifecycle Method	Purpose
componentDidMount	Executes **after** the component is added to the DOM (e.g., fetching API data).
componentDidUpdate	Runs when state/props **change** (e.g., updating UI after data change).
componentWillUnmount	Cleans up before the component is removed (e.g., **removing event listeners**).

javascript

Example:

```
componentDidMount() {
  console.log('Component mounted!');
}
```

4. React Hooks (For Functional Components)

What are React Hooks? Why Were They Introduced?

- Hooks **allow functional components to use state and lifecycle features** without writing class components.

Explain useState with an Example

javascript

Example:

```
import React, { useState } from 'react';


const Counter = () => {

  const [count, setCount] = useState(0);

  return <button onClick={() => setCount(count + 1)}>Count: {count}</button>;

};
```

How Does useEffect Work? Provide Real-World Examples.

- useEffect runs **side effects** in functional components.

javascript

Example:

```
useEffect(() => {

  console.log('Component Mounted');

  return () => console.log('Component Unmounted');

}, []);
```

5. React Interview Questions on State Management

What is State in React, and How is it Managed?

- State is **component-specific data** that can change over time.

When Should We Use Context API Instead of Redux?

- Use **Context API** for **small applications** with minimal state.
  Use **Redux** for **large-scale applications** needing **centralized state management**.

---

6. Virtual DOM and Reconciliation

What is the Virtual DOM, and How Does It Improve Performance?

- React's **Virtual DOM** is an in-memory representation of the **actual DOM**, reducing direct DOM manipulations.

What Are React Keys, and Why Are They Important?

- Keys **help React identify elements efficiently**.

javascript

Example:

```
items.map((item) => <li key={item.id}>{item.name}</li>);
```

---

7. React Router and Navigation

How Does React Router Work?

- React Router **enables client-side navigation** without full-page reloads.

javascript

Example:

import { BrowserRouter, Route, Switch } from 'react-router-dom';

```
<BrowserRouter>
  <Switch>
    <Route path="/" component={Home} exact />
    <Route path="/about" component={About} />
  </Switch>
</BrowserRouter>
```

8. React Interview Questions on Performance Optimization

How Does React Lazy Loading Work?

- Lazy loading **dynamically imports components** only when needed.

javascript

Example:

```
import React, { lazy, Suspense } from 'react';

const LazyComponent = lazy(() => import('./LazyComponent'));

<Suspense fallback={<p>Loading...</p>}>
  <LazyComponent />
```

```
</Suspense>;
```

---

9. Event Handling in React

How Does Event Binding Work in React?

Binding events inside a constructor:

javascript

Example:

```
constructor() {
  this.handleClick = this.handleClick.bind(this);
}
```

- Using **arrow functions** to avoid explicit binding:

javascript

Example:

```
<button onClick={() => this.handleClick()}>Click Me</button>
```

---

10. Controlled vs. Uncontrolled Components

• Feature	• Controlled Component	• Uncontrolled Component
State Management	Handled by React	Managed by the DOM
Example Usage	Forms, Inputs	File Uploads

- **Example of a Controlled Component:**

javascript

Example:

```javascript
const [text, setText] = useState("");
<input value={text} onChange={(e) => setText(e.target.value)} />;
```

---

11. Error Handling in React

What Are Error Boundaries in React?

- Error boundaries **catch runtime errors** and prevent app crashes.

javascript

Example:

```javascript
class ErrorBoundary extends React.Component {
  state = { hasError: false };

  static getDerivedStateFromError() {
    return { hasError: true };
  }

  render() {
    return this.state.hasError ? <h1>Something went wrong</h1> : this.props.children;
  }
}
```

---

12. Conclusion and Best Practices

Best Practices for Writing Clean React Code

- Use **functional components with hooks.**
- Optimize with **React.memo & useMemo.**
- Use **Error Boundaries** to handle errors.
- Follow **component-based architecture** for reusability.

How to Prepare for React.js Interviews Effectively

- **Practice hands-on coding** for components, hooks, and state management.
- **Understand React internals** (Virtual DOM, reconciliation, event system).
- **Review common interview questions** and **solve real-world problems.**

CHAPTER 9

Advanced React Concepts

1. Introduction to Advanced React Concepts

- As React applications grow in complexity, mastering **advanced concepts** becomes essential for building **high-performance, scalable, and maintainable** applications. Companies like **Facebook, Netflix, and Airbnb** leverage React's advanced capabilities to optimize user experiences.

Why Are Advanced React Concepts Important for MNC Interviews?

MNCs expect developers to:

- **Write optimized, scalable React applications.**
- **Understand the Virtual DOM, reconciliation, and rendering optimizations.**
- **Efficiently manage application state and handle side effects.**
- **Implement server-side rendering (SSR) and concurrent rendering.**
- This chapter will explore these key areas, equipping you with expert-level knowledge to **ace MNC technical interviews.**

2. Higher-Order Components (HOCs)

What Are Higher-Order Components?

- A **Higher-Order Component (HOC)** is a function that takes a component as input and returns a new enhanced component.
- **Purpose of HOCs:**
- **Code reuse** – Encapsulates logic used across multiple components.
- **Separation of concerns** – Keeps UI components clean.
- **Enhancing components dynamically** – Adds authentication, logging, or styling.

Example: Implementing an Authentication HOC

javascript

Example:

import React from 'react';

```javascript
const withAuth = (WrappedComponent) => {
  return (props) => {
    const isAuthenticated = localStorage.getItem('token');

    return isAuthenticated ? <WrappedComponent {...props} /> :
<p>Access Denied</p>;
  };
};


const Dashboard = () => <h1>Welcome to Dashboard</h1>;


export default withAuth(Dashboard);
```

Common Mistakes with HOCs

- **Unnecessary re-renders** – Optimize with React.memo().
- **Not forwarding refs** – Use React.forwardRef().

3. React Performance Optimization

Common Performance Bottlenecks

- **Unnecessary re-renders** due to state changes.
- **Excessive API calls** inside useEffect().
- **Large bundle sizes** slowing down page load.

Optimizing Functional Components with React.memo()

React.memo() prevents re-renders if props remain unchanged.

javascript

Example:

```
const MemoizedComponent = React.memo(({ value }) =>
<p>{value}</p>);
```

Using useMemo() and useCallback()

- useMemo() – **Caching Expensive Computations**

javascript

Example:

```
const result = useMemo(() => expensiveFunction(data), [data]);
```

- useCallback() – **Prevents Unnecessary Function Recreation**

javascript

Example:

```
const handleClick = useCallback(() => console.log('Clicked'), []);
```

Profiling Performance Using React DevTools

- React DevTools can help **identify slow components** and **optimize renders**.

---

4. Server-Side Rendering (SSR) vs Client-Side Rendering (CSR)

Feature	SSR	CSR
Rendering	On the server before reaching the browser	In the browser using JavaScript
Performance	Faster initial load	Slower initial load
SEO	Better for SEO	Less SEO-friendly

Implementing SSR Using Next.js

javascript

Example:

```javascript
export async function getServerSideProps() {
  const data = await fetchAPI();
  return { props: { data } };
}


const Page = ({ data }) => <p>{data}</p>;
export default Page;
```

5. Virtual DOM and Reconciliation

How Does React's Virtual DOM Improve Performance?

- **Minimizes direct DOM manipulations.**
- **Uses a diffing algorithm to detect changes.**
- **Efficiently updates only modified elements.**

What Are React Keys and Why Are They Important?

- Keys help React efficiently **identify** which items changed, added, or removed in lists.

javascript

Example:

```javascript
items.map(item => <li key={item.id}>{item.name}</li>);
```

---

6. Lazy Loading and Code Splitting

What Is Lazy Loading?

- Lazy loading **reduces initial bundle size** by loading components **only when needed.**

Using React.lazy() and Suspense

javascript

Example:

```javascript
import React, { lazy, Suspense } from 'react';


const LazyComponent = lazy(() => import('./LazyComponent'));


<Suspense fallback={<p>Loading...</p>}>
  <LazyComponent />
```

```
</Suspense>;
```

Optimizing Code Splitting with React Router

javascript

Example:

```
const LazyPage = lazy(() => import('./Page'));


<Route            path="/page"            element={<Suspense
fallback={<p>Loading...</p>}><LazyPage /></Suspense>} />
```

7. Concurrent Rendering and React Fiber

What Is React Fiber?

- React Fiber is a **reconciliation engine** that improves rendering performance **by splitting tasks into smaller chunks**.

Using Suspense for Concurrent Rendering

javascript

Example:

```
<Suspense fallback={<Loading />}>
  <Component />
</Suspense>
```

8. Handling Side Effects Efficiently

Common Mistakes with useEffect()

- **Calling APIs without a dependency array** – Leads to infinite loops.
- **Using setState inside useEffect() incorrectly.**

Best Practices for Handling API Calls

javascript

Example:

```javascript
useEffect(() => {
  let isMounted = true;
  fetchData().then(data => isMounted && setData(data));
  return () => isMounted = false;
}, []);
```

9. Error Boundaries in React

What Are Error Boundaries?

- Error boundaries **catch JavaScript errors** in components and prevent crashes.

Implementing an Error Boundary

javascript

Example:

```javascript
class ErrorBoundary extends React.Component {
  state = { hasError: false };

  static getDerivedStateFromError() {
    return { hasError: true };
  }
```

```
render() {

  return this.state.hasError ? <h1>Something went wrong.</
h1> : this.props.children;

  }
}
```

10. Custom Hooks in React

Why Use Custom Hooks?

- **Encapsulate reusable logic.**
- **Improve code readability and maintainability.**

Implementing a useFetch Custom Hook

javascript

Example:

```
const useFetch = (url) => {
  const [data, setData] = useState(null);


  useEffect(() => {
    fetch(url).then(res => res.json()).then(setData);
  }, [url]);


  return data;
};
```

11. Advanced State Management Techniques

When to Use Context API vs Redux?

Use Case	Context API	Redux
Local state management	Suitable	Not recommended
Large-scale applications	Not ideal	Preferred
Performance optimization	Limited	More efficient

Optimizing State Management with Redux Toolkit

javascript

Example:

```javascript
import { createSlice } from '@reduxjs/toolkit';

const counterSlice = createSlice({
  name: 'counter',
  initialState: 0,
  reducers: {
    increment: state => state + 1,
    decrement: state => state - 1
  }
});

export const { increment, decrement } = counterSlice.actions;
export default counterSlice.reducer;
```

12. Conclusion and Interview Tips

Key Takeaways

- Optimize components with React.memo(), useMemo(), and useCallback().
- Use Suspense for concurrent rendering.
- Leverage useEffect correctly to handle side effects.
- Implement SSR with Next.js for SEO benefits.

Common React Interview Questions on Advanced Topics

- How does React optimize rendering performance?
- What are the benefits of React Fiber?
- How do you implement lazy loading in React?
- Explain the difference between Context API and Redux.
- What are best practices for handling API calls in useEffect()?

Best Resources for Mastering Advanced React

- React Docs: https://react.dev
- "Full-Stack React Projects" by Shama Hoque
- React DevTools for performance profiling

CHAPTER 10

State Management in React

1. Introduction to State Management in React

What is State Management?

- State management in React refers to how data is stored, updated, and shared across components in an application. React's **state system** is essential for creating dynamic and interactive user interfaces.

Why is State Management Crucial in React Applications?

- **Maintains UI Consistency** – Ensures that all components display the correct data.
- **Optimizes Performance** – Prevents unnecessary re-renders and improves efficiency.
- **Manages Complex Interactions** – Helps handle asynchronous data fetching, user authentication, and global application state.

Common Problems Without a Proper State Management Strategy

- **Prop Drilling:** Passing state through multiple levels of components, making code harder to maintain.
- **Redundant State:** Multiple components storing the same data, leading to inconsistencies.
- **Difficult Debugging:** Tracking changes in an unstructured state can cause unexpected bugs.

State Management Techniques in React

- React provides various ways to manage state, ranging from **local state** within components to **global state** for application-wide data.

  - **State Management Approach**

    - **Description**

      - **Use Case**

  - **useState**

Manages local component state.

   Small-scale applications, simple states.

  - **useReducer**

Manages complex state logic.

   When state updates depend on previous values.

  - **Context API**

Provides global state management.

   Sharing data between multiple components.

  - **Redux**

Centralized state management with a store.

   Large applications needing predictable state updates.

- **Redux Toolkit**

Simplified Redux with less boilerplate.

Modern React-Redux applications.

2. When to Use State Management Libraries

Built-in React State Management (useState, useContext) vs Third-Party Solutions

• Feature	• useState & useContext	• Redux & Redux Toolkit
• Complexity	Simple to use	More setup required
• Performance	Efficient for small apps	Optimized for large apps
• Scalability	Limited	Ideal for enterprise apps
• Boilerplate	Minimal	Requires actions, reducers, middleware

When to Use Redux or Other Libraries

- Use **React's built-in state management** for simple applications or component-specific states.
- Use **Redux or Context API** when multiple components require shared state.
- Use **Redux Toolkit** for scalable, production-grade state management.

3. Understanding useState and useReducer

Managing Local State with useState

javascript

Example:

```javascript
import React, { useState } from 'react';


const Counter = () => {
  const [count, setCount] = useState(0);


  return (
    <button onClick={() => setCount(count + 1)}>
      Count: {count}
    </button>
  );
};
export default Counter;
```

Limitations of useState

- **Difficult to manage complex state logic** (e.g., deeply nested objects).
- **Frequent state updates cause unnecessary re-renders.**

Using useReducer for Complex State Logic

javascript

Example:

```javascript
import React, { useReducer } from 'react';
```

```
const reducer = (state, action) => {
  switch (action.type) {
    case 'increment': return { count: state.count + 1 };
    case 'decrement': return { count: state.count - 1 };
    default: return state;
  }
};


const Counter = () => {
  const [state, dispatch] = useReducer(reducer, { count: 0 });


  return (
    <div>
      <button onClick={() => dispatch({ type: 'increment' })}>+</button>
      <p>{state.count}</p>
      <button onClick={() => dispatch({ type: 'decrement' })}>-</button>
    </div>
  );
};
export default Counter;
```

Comparing useState and useReducer

- **useState** is simpler for **single-value states**.
- **useReducer** is better for **complex state logic** requiring multiple updates.

---

4. Managing Global State with Context API

Why Use Context API?

- The Context API allows **global state management** without prop drilling.

Example: Using Context API for Theme Management

javascript

Example:

```
import React, { createContext, useState, useContext } from 'react';


const ThemeContext = createContext();


const ThemeProvider = ({ children }) => {
  const [theme, setTheme] = useState('light');
  return (
    <ThemeContext.Provider value={{ theme, setTheme }}>
      {children}
    </ThemeContext.Provider>
  );
};


const ThemedComponent = () => {
```

```
const { theme, setTheme } = useContext(ThemeContext);

return (

  <button onClick={() => setTheme(theme === 'light' ? 'dark' :
'light')}>

    Toggle Theme (Current: {theme})

  </button>

);

};


export default function App() {

  return (

    <ThemeProvider>

      <ThemedComponent />

    </ThemeProvider>

  );

}
```

5. Introduction to Redux for State Management

Core Concepts of Redux

- **Store:** Centralized state container.
- **Actions:** Events that describe state changes.
- **Reducers:** Pure functions that update the state.

Setting Up Redux in a React Application

javascript

Example:

```
import { createStore } from 'redux';


const reducer = (state = { count: 0 }, action) => {
  switch (action.type) {
    case 'increment': return { count: state.count + 1 };
    default: return state;
  }
};


const store = createStore(reducer);
```

---

6. Using Redux Toolkit for Simplified State Management

Why Use Redux Toolkit?

- **Less boilerplate** than traditional Redux.
- **Built-in support for asynchronous state management.**

Example: Setting Up Redux Toolkit

javascript

Example:

```
import { createSlice, configureStore } from '@reduxjs/toolkit';


const counterSlice = createSlice({
  name: 'counter',
  initialState: 0,
```

```
reducers: {
  increment: state => state + 1,
 }
});
```

```
export const { increment } = counterSlice.actions;
const store = configureStore({ reducer: counterSlice.reducer });
```

7. Managing API Calls with Redux Thunk and Redux Saga

Redux Thunk (Handling Side Effects)

javascript

Example:

```
import { createAsyncThunk } from '@reduxjs/toolkit';
```

```
export const fetchData = createAsyncThunk('data/fetch', async
() => {
  const response = await fetch('/api/data');
  return response.json();
});
```

8. Optimizing State Management in React Applications

- **Use useMemo() to prevent unnecessary recalculations.**

- Use React.memo() to prevent unnecessary re-renders.
- Split global and local state efficiently.

9. Best Practices for Scalable State Management

- Organize Redux store properly (reducers, actions, selectors).
- Use selectors for efficient data access.
- Implement lazy loading to optimize performance.

10. Common State Management Interview Questions

1. What is the difference between local state and global state?

- **Local state** is managed within a single component, while **global state** is shared across multiple components.

2. When should you use Redux instead of Context API?

- Use **Redux** when dealing with **large applications**, complex state logic, or frequent updates.

3. How do you optimize a Redux-based application?

- Use **Redux Toolkit** to reduce boilerplate.
- Use **memoization** with selectors.

11. Conclusion and Key Takeaways

- Use Context API for moderate state sharing.
- Use Redux for complex, large-scale applications.
- Use Redux Toolkit to simplify Redux implementations.
- Optimize performance using memoization techniques.

CHAPTER 11

Building a Full-Stack MERN Application

1. Introduction to Full-Stack MERN Applications

Overview of Full-Stack Development

- Full-stack development refers to building both the **frontend (client-side)** and **backend (server-side)** of an application, allowing developers to create complete, functional web applications. A full-stack developer is responsible for handling **database management, backend logic, API development, UI design, and client-server communication**.

Why Use the MERN Stack for Modern Web Applications?

- The **MERN stack** consists of four technologies that work seamlessly together:
- **MongoDB** – A NoSQL database that stores data in flexible JSON-like documents.
- **Express.js** – A lightweight Node.js framework for building APIs.
- **React.js** – A frontend library for building interactive UIs.
- **Node.js** – A JavaScript runtime that runs on the server.

Advantages of the MERN Stack Over Other Stacks

- **Full JavaScript Stack:** Uses JavaScript/TypeScript for both frontend and backend, reducing context switching.
- **Fast Development:** React's component-based architecture speeds up UI development.
- **Scalability:** MongoDB's flexible schema and Express.js' lightweight nature allow building scalable applications.
- **Strong Community Support:** Large open-source ecosystem with numerous libraries and tools.

2. Setting Up the Development Environment

Installing Node.js and MongoDB

- **Install Node.js** (LTS recommended) from nodejs.org
  bash
  Example:

```
node -v # Check version

  npm -v  # Check npm version
```

- **Install MongoDB** from mongodb.com
  bash
  Example:

```
mongod --version # Check MongoDB version
```

Setting Up an Express.js Backend

bash

Example:

```
mkdir mern-app && cd mern-app

npm init -y

npm install express mongoose dotenv cors jsonwebtoken bcryptjs
```

Creating a React Application Using Vite

bash

Example:

npm create vite@latest client --template react

cd client

npm install

Project Structure for Scalability

arduino

Example:

```
mern-app/
|── backend/
|     ├── models/
|     ├── routes/
|     ├── controllers/
|     ├── middleware/
|     ├── config/
|     ├── server.js
|── client/
|     ├── src/
|     |    ├── components/
|     |    ├── pages/
|     |    ├── context/
|     |    ├── App.js
```

3. Backend Development with Node.js and Express.js

Setting Up Express.js and Creating API Routes

javascript

Example:

```javascript
const express = require('express');
const dotenv = require('dotenv');
const cors = require('cors');
const mongoose = require('mongoose');

dotenv.config();
const app = express();

app.use(express.json());
app.use(cors());

app.get('/', (req, res) => res.send('API is running'));

const PORT = process.env.PORT || 5000;
app.listen(PORT, () => console.log(`Server running on port ${PORT}`));
```

Connecting to MongoDB Using Mongoose

javascript

Example:

```javascript
const mongoose = require('mongoose');

mongoose.connect(process.env.MONGO_URI, {
    useNewUrlParser: true,
    useUnifiedTopology: true,
})
.then(() => console.log('MongoDB Connected'))
.catch(err => console.log(err));
```

Implementing CRUD Operations

- Example **User Model:**

javascript

Example:

```javascript
const mongoose = require('mongoose');

const userSchema = new mongoose.Schema({
    name: String,
    email: String,
    password: String
});

module.exports = mongoose.model('User', userSchema);
```

- Example **Create User API Route:**

javascript

Example:

```
const express = require('express');
const User = require('../models/User');


const router = express.Router();


router.post('/register', async (req, res) => {
    const { name, email, password } = req.body;
    const user = new User({ name, email, password });
    await user.save();
    res.status(201).json(user);
});


module.exports = router;
```

Handling Authentication Using JWT

javascript

Example:

```
const jwt = require('jsonwebtoken');


const generateToken = (id) => {
    return jwt.sign({ id }, process.env.JWT_SECRET, { expiresIn:
'30d' });
};
```

4. Frontend Development with React.js

Setting Up the React Project Structure

- components/ – Reusable UI components.
- pages/ – Page-level components (e.g., Home, Dashboard).
- context/ – Context API for global state management.

Fetching Data from Backend Using Axios

bash

Example:

```
npm install axios
```

javascript

Example:

```
import axios from 'axios';

const fetchUsers = async () => {
    const response = await axios.get('http://localhost:5000/api/users');
    console.log(response.data);
};
```

Implementing Authentication and Protected Routes

javascript

Example:

```
import { Navigate } from 'react-router-dom';
```

```
const PrivateRoute = ({ children }) => {
    return  localStorage.getItem('token') ? children : <Navigate
to="/login" />;
};
```

---

5. Integrating Frontend and Backend

Handling CORS Issues and Configuring Proxy

javascript

Example:

```
app.use(cors({ origin: 'http://localhost:3000' }));
```

Error Handling and Debugging

- Use **React DevTools** to debug UI issues.
- Use **Postman** for API testing.
- Implement **error handling middleware** in Express.

---

6. Optimizing Performance and Scalability

Optimizing MongoDB Queries

javascript

Example:

```
User.find().select('-password').lean();
```

Using React Memoization Techniques

javascript

Example:

```
import React, { useMemo } from 'react';


const MemoizedComponent = React.memo((({ value }) => {
    return <p>{value}</p>;
});
```

Implementing Pagination

javascript

Example:

```
const users = await User.find().limit(10).skip(10 * page);
```

---

7. Security Best Practices

Protecting API Endpoints

javascript

Example:

```
const authMiddleware = (req, res, next) => {
    const token = req.headers.authorization.split(' ')[1];
    jwt.verify(token, process.env.JWT_SECRET, (err, user) => {
        if (err) return res.status(403).json('Invalid token');
        req.user = user;
        next();
    });
};
```

Using Environment Variables for Sensitive Information

bash

Example:

MONGO_URI=your_mongodb_connection_string

JWT_SECRET=your_secret_key

---

8. Testing the Application

- **Unit Tests:** Jest and Mocha.
- **API Tests:** Postman and Supertest.
- **E2E Tests:** Cypress.

Example API Test:

```
const request = require('supertest');
const app = require('../server');


describe('GET /api/users', () => {
   it('should return a list of users', async () => {
      const res = await request(app).get('/api/users');
      expect(res.status).toBe(200);
   });
});
```

---

9. Deploying the MERN Application

Deploying the Backend

- **Heroku:** git push heroku main
- **AWS EC2:** Using Docker containers.

Deploying the Frontend

- **Netlify/Vercel:** npm run build → Upload build/ folder.

Configuring CI/CD Pipelines

yaml

Example:

name: CI/CD Pipeline

on: push

jobs:

  build:

    runs-on: ubuntu-latest

    steps:

      - name: Checkout repository

        uses: actions/checkout@v2

      - name: Install dependencies

        run: npm install

      - name: Run tests

        run: npm test

10. Conclusion and Best Practices

- **Follow modular architecture for scalability.**
- **Use middleware for security and performance.**
- **Optimize API calls with caching.**
- **Implement CI/CD for automated deployments.**

CHAPTER 12

Database Design and Optimization for MERN Stack Applications

1. Introduction to Database Design

Importance of Efficient Database Design in Full-Stack Applications

- Database design plays a crucial role in the **scalability, performance, and maintainability** of full-stack applications. Poorly structured databases lead to slow queries, inefficient storage, and difficulties in handling growing datasets. A well-designed database:
- Reduces **data redundancy** and improves **data integrity**.
- Ensures **faster query execution** with proper indexing.
- Helps in **scaling** efficiently with sharding and replication.
- Simplifies **data relationships** in complex applications.

Key Differences Between SQL and NoSQL Databases

- **Feature**

    - **SQL (Relational)**

        - **NoSQL (MongoDB)**

- **Data Model**

Structured, tabular data

Flexible, JSON-like documents

- **Schema**

Fixed schema, predefined tables

Schema-less, dynamic structure

- **Joins**

Supports complex joins

No joins, relies on embedding/referencing

- **Scalability**

Vertical (adding more CPU/RAM)

Horizontal (sharding across servers)

- **Use Cases**

Banking, ERP, CRM

Real-time apps, e-commerce, IoT

Why MongoDB is Preferred in the MERN Stack

- **JSON-Like Documents:** MongoDB's BSON format matches JavaScript objects, making integration with Node.js seamless.

- **Flexible Schema:** Ideal for handling **rapidly evolving** application data structures.
- **Scalability:** Supports **horizontal scaling (sharding)** for handling high-traffic applications.
- **Performance:** Fast read/write operations due to **indexing** and **document-based storage**.

Best Practices for Designing a Scalable Database Schema

- **Define clear data models** before coding.
- **Use indexing** for frequently queried fields.
- **Embed data** when relationships are tightly coupled.
- **Use references** when dealing with large, independent datasets.
- **Optimize query patterns** for performance and scalability.

2. Structuring a MongoDB Database for MERN Applications

Understanding Collections, Documents, and Fields

- **Collections** – Equivalent to tables in SQL, groups of related documents.
- **Documents** – JSON-like objects containing data (equivalent to rows in SQL).
- **Fields** – Individual data points within a document (equivalent to columns in SQL).
- Example of a **User Document** in MongoDB:

json

Example:

```
{
  "_id": "617f1f77bcf86cd799439012",
  "name": "John Doe",
  "email": "johndoe@example.com",
```

```
"orders": [
  { "orderId": "12345", "amount": 99.99, "status": "shipped" }
]
}
```

Schema Design Patterns in MongoDB

- **Single Table (Denormalized) Approach** – Embeds related data directly in a document.
- **Normalized Approach** – Uses references to avoid redundant data.

Normalization vs. Denormalization in NoSQL Databases

- **Approach**

  - **Advantages**

    - **Disadvantages**

  - **Embedding (Denormalization)**

  Faster reads, less querying overhead

    Data duplication, risk of large document sizes

  - **Referencing (Normalization)**

  Avoids redundancy, maintains consistency

    Slower queries requiring joins

Handling Relationships in MongoDB

- **One-to-One:** Store embedded documents if data is

frequently accessed together.
- **One-to-Many:** Use **arrays** for small lists, references for larger datasets.
- **Many-to-Many:** Use linking collections with references.
- Example: **One-to-Many using References**

json

Example:

```
{
  "_id": "617f1f77bcf86cd799439012",
  "name": "John Doe",
  "email": "johndoe@example.com",
  "orders": ["orderId_123", "orderId_124"]
}
```

---

3. Indexing Strategies for Performance Optimization

What Are Indexes in MongoDB and Why Are They Important?

- Indexes speed up queries by **reducing the number of documents MongoDB scans**. Without indexes, MongoDB performs a **full collection scan**, leading to poor performance.

Types of Indexes in MongoDB

- **Single Field Index** – Indexes a single field.
  javascript
  Example:
  ```javascript
  db.users.createIndex({ email: 1 });
  ```
- **Compound Index** – Indexes multiple fields.

javascript
Example:
db.orders.createIndex({ userId: 1, createdAt: -1 });

- **Multikey Index** – Indexes array values.
- **Text Index** – Used for **full-text search**.
- **Geospatial Index** – Used for **location-based queries**.

Measuring Index Performance Using explain()

javascript

Example:

db.orders.find({ userId:
"617f1f77bcf86cd799439012" }).explain("executionStats");

4. Query Optimization Techniques

Writing Efficient Queries to Improve Performance

- **Use projections** to retrieve only necessary fields.
  javascript
  Example:
  db.users.find({}, { name: 1, email: 1 });
- **Avoid $regex on large datasets** (use full-text search instead).
- **Use limit() and skip() for pagination** to reduce query load.

Using Aggregation Pipelines for Complex Queries

javascript

Example:

db.orders.aggregate([

  { $match: { status: "shipped" } },

  { $group: { _id: "$userId", totalSpent: { $sum: "$amount" } } }

]);

5. Handling Large Data Sets in MongoDB

Sharding Strategies for Distributing Data

- **Range-Based Sharding:** Data is split by a defined range of values.
- **Hash-Based Sharding:** Uses a hash function to distribute data evenly.
- **Zone-Based Sharding:** Routes data based on geographic zones.

Pagination Techniques

javascript

Example:

```
db.products.find().sort({ createdAt: -1 }).skip(20).limit(10);
```

6. Caching Strategies for Faster Query Execution

- **Use Redis for caching frequently accessed queries.**
- **Invalidate cache on database updates to prevent stale data.**
- Example: **Using Redis with Node.js**

javascript

Example:

```
const redis = require('redis');
const client = redis.createClient();


const fetchUsers = async () => {
  const cachedUsers = await client.get("users");
```

```javascript
  if (cachedUsers) return JSON.parse(cachedUsers);

  const users = await User.find();
  client.setex("users", 3600, JSON.stringify(users));
  return users;
};
```

---

7. Transactions and Data Integrity in MongoDB

Multi-Document Transactions

javascript

Example:

```javascript
const session = await mongoose.startSession();
session.startTransaction();

try {
    await User.updateOne({ _id: userId }, { $inc: { balance: -100 } },
{ session });
    await Order.create([{ userId, amount: 100 }], { session });
    await session.commitTransaction();
} catch (error) {
    await session.abortTransaction();
} finally {
    session.endSession();
}
```

8. Best Practices for Securing MongoDB Databases

- Enable authentication and role-based access control (RBAC).
- Encrypt sensitive data using MongoDB's field-level encryption.
- Use .env files to store database credentials securely.

9. Backup and Recovery Strategies

- Automated Backups using MongoDB Atlas.
- Restore from backups using mongorestore.
- Implement replication for high availability.

10. Conclusion and Key Takeaways

- Design scalable schemas with proper indexing strategies.
- Use aggregation pipelines for efficient data processing.
- Implement caching to speed up frequently accessed queries.
- Secure MongoDB with proper authentication and encryption.

CHAPTER 13

System Design Questions for MERN Stack

1. Introduction to System Design in MERN Stack

What is System Design and Why is it Important?

- System design refers to **architecting scalable, efficient, and maintainable applications** by considering components like **databases, caching, APIs, microservices, security, and fault tolerance**. In the MERN (MongoDB, Express.js, React, Node.js) stack, system design ensures the application can handle **high traffic, concurrency, and performance bottlenecks**.

Why Do MNCs Focus on System Design Interviews for MERN Developers?

- MNCs conduct **system design interviews** to evaluate a candidate's ability to:
- **Build scalable applications** that can handle large user bases.
- **Optimize performance** through caching, database design, and efficient API handling.
- **Ensure maintainability and modularity** through proper architectural decisions.
- **Implement security best practices** to protect user data and prevent attacks.

Key System Design Components

- **Component**
- **Description**

- **Scalability** — How well the system handles increasing traffic and data load.

- **Performance** — Speed of responses, database queries, and API calls.

- **Maintainability** — Code modularity, separation of concerns, and ease of updates.

- **Fault Tolerance** — System's ability to handle failures and recover automatically.

- **Security** — Authentication, authorization, data encryption, and protection from attacks.

2. Key System Design Concepts in MERN Stack

Scalability: Vertical vs. Horizontal Scaling

- **Vertical Scaling:** Increasing resources (CPU, RAM) on a single server.
- **Horizontal Scaling:** Adding more servers to distribute the load.
- MERN applications benefit from **horizontal scaling** using **load balancers** and **database sharding**.

Load Balancing Strategies for High-Traffic Applications

Load balancers distribute incoming requests across multiple servers to prevent overload.

- **Common Load Balancing Techniques:**
- **Round Robin:** Evenly distributes traffic among servers.
- **Least Connections:** Sends requests to the server with the fewest active connections.
- **IP Hashing:** Assigns users to specific servers for session persistence.
- **Example Load Balancer (Nginx):**

nginx

Example:

```
upstream backend {
    server app1.example.com;
    server app2.example.com;
}
server {
    location / {
        proxy_pass http://backend;
    }
}
```

Caching Mechanisms for Performance Optimization

- **Redis:** Stores frequently accessed database queries.
- **CDN:** Caches static assets (CSS, JS, images) globally.
- **In-Memory Caching:** Reduces direct database queries.

Database Optimization Techniques for MongoDB

- **Use Indexes:** Speed up query execution.
- **Aggregation Pipelines:** Process large data sets efficiently.
- **Partitioning & Sharding:** Distribute data across multiple servers.

Asynchronous Processing with Message Queues

- **RabbitMQ/Kafka** helps handle **background tasks** like email notifications.
- Reduces **blocking API responses** and improves **system performance**.
- **Example: Using Bull.js for Queue Processing**

javascript

Example:

```
const Queue = require('bull');

const emailQueue = new Queue('email');


emailQueue.process(async (job) => {

    console.log(`Sending email to ${job.data.email}`);
});
```

3. Designing a Scalable E-Commerce Platform Using MERN

Step-by-Step Breakdown of E-Commerce System Design

- o **Frontend (React.js)**

- o User authentication (JWT/OAuth).
- o Product listing with pagination.
- o Cart management and order placement.
- o **Backend (Express.js & Node.js)**

- o REST API for product management.
- o Secure payment gateway integration.
- o User authentication and order tracking.

○ **Database (MongoDB)**

    i. **Products Collection:** Stores product details.

    ii. **Users Collection:** Manages authentication.

    iii. **Orders Collection:** Tracks purchases.

Database Schema Design

javascript

Example:

```javascript
const orderSchema = new mongoose.Schema({
    userId: { type: mongoose.Schema.Types.ObjectId, ref: 'User' },
    items: [{ productId: String, quantity: Number }],
    totalAmount: Number,
    status: { type: String, enum: ['pending', 'shipped', 'delivered'] }
});
```

Handling High Concurrency in E-Commerce

- **Optimistic Locking:** Prevents overselling.
- **Rate Limiting:** Prevents API abuse using **Express Rate Limit**.
- **Database Read Replicas:** Reduces load on the primary database.

4. Handling Millions of Concurrent Users in a MERN Application

- **Use Nginx/AWS Load Balancers** to distribute traffic.
- **Leverage Redis for session storage and caching.**
- **Use Database Replication** to scale read-heavy queries.

Rate Limiting and Throttling

javascript

Example:

```
const rateLimit = require('express-rate-limit');
app.use(rateLimit({ windowMs: 1 * 60 * 1000, max: 100 }));
```

5. Best Practices for Caching and Performance Optimization

- **Technique**
- **Purpose**

- **Redis Cache**   Store frequently accessed data to reduce DB queries.

- **CDN**   Load static assets quickly.

- **MongoDB Indexing**   Optimize search queries.

- **Compression (Gzip)**   Reduce payload size for faster transfers.

6. Microservices vs Monolithic Architecture for MERN Applications

- **Feature**
  - **Monolithic**
    - **Microservices**
- **Scalability**

Limited

Highly scalable

- **Deployment**

Entire app redeployed

Independent service deployment

- **Maintenance**

Harder in large apps

Easier to maintain

Communication in Microservices

- **REST APIs:** Standard approach but can have latency.
- **GraphQL:** Fetch only required data, reducing network load.
- **gRPC:** High-performance communication between services.

7. Real-World Case Study: Scaling a MERN-Based SaaS Application

- A SaaS application initially built as a monolith faced **latency issues** with 1M+ users. **Solution:**
- **Split Monolith into Microservices** (User Service, Billing Service).
- **Implemented Redis & CDN** for caching.
- **Used Kubernetes for Load Balancing** and Auto-scaling.

8. Common System Design Interview Questions for MERN Developers

1. How would you design a high-traffic social media application using MERN?

- **Key Points:**
- Use **CDN** for static files.
- Implement **database sharding** for user data.
- Optimize **real-time feeds** with WebSockets and Redis.

2. How would you handle real-time notifications in a MERN app?

- **Solution:**
- Use **WebSockets (Socket.io)** for instant updates.
- Store notifications in **MongoDB** for retrieval.
- Use **RabbitMQ for async event processing.**

9. Conclusion and Final Tips

Recap of Key System Design Principles

- Use **load balancers** for distributing traffic.
- Optimize **MongoDB queries** for performance.
- Implement **microservices for scalable architectures.**
- Use **caching techniques (Redis, CDN)** for faster responses.

Final Tips for System Design Interviews

- **Clarify requirements** before designing the system.
- **Consider trade-offs** (e.g., Monolithic vs. Microservices).
- **Use diagrams** to explain architecture.
- **Think about scalability and fault tolerance.**

Recommended Resources

- **"Designing Data-Intensive Applications" by Martin Kleppmann**
- **"System Design Interview" by Alex Xu**
- **MongoDB University: Performance Tuning Courses**

CHAPTER 14

Real-Time Applications with MERN Stack

1. Introduction to Real-Time Applications

What Are Real-Time Applications?

- Real-time applications (RTAs) provide **instant data updates** to users **without requiring manual refreshes**. These applications create an interactive user experience by enabling **bidirectional communication between clients and servers**.

Why Are Real-Time Applications Important?

- Real-time applications are crucial for **modern web experiences**, where users expect **instant updates**. Key benefits include:
- **Enhanced User Engagement:** Instant feedback loops increase user interaction.
- **Improved Collaboration:** Multi-user systems like Google Docs rely on real-time sync.
- **Efficient Data Processing:** Live monitoring and analytics depend on instant data updates.

Common Use Cases of Real-Time Applications

- **Use Case**
- **Description**

- **Chat Applications** Messaging apps like WhatsApp and Slack provide instant communication.

- **Live Notifications** Real-time alerts in social media and financial applications.

- **Collaborative Tools** Platforms like Google Docs enable multiple users to edit in real time.

- **Live Streaming** Streaming platforms like YouTube Live and Twitch.

- **Online Gaming** Multiplayer online games require real-time synchronization.

How Do Real-Time Applications Differ from Traditional Web Applications?

Feature	Traditional Web Apps	Real-Time Apps
Data Updates	Requires manual refresh	Push-based live updates
Communication	Client initiates requests	Server pushes updates proactively
Latency	High latency	Low latency
Use Cases	Blogs, static websites	Chat apps, live dashboards

2. WebSockets and Real-Time Communication

What Are WebSockets and How Do They Work?

- **WebSockets** are a protocol that allows **persistent, bidirectional communication** between a client and a server. Unlike HTTP, WebSockets remain **open**, enabling real-time data transfer.
- **How WebSockets Work:**
- **Handshake** – The client initiates a connection to the server.
- **Persistent Connection** – A single TCP connection remains open.
- **Bidirectional Communication** – The client and server send messages to each other.

WebSockets vs. Traditional HTTP Requests

Feature	WebSockets	HTTP Requests
Connection	Persistent	Stateless
Data Flow	Bidirectional	Request-response
Efficiency	High (low overhead)	Less efficient for real-time use cases

Real-Time Communication Protocols

- **Protocol**
  - **Description**
    - **Use Case**
- **WebSockets**

Full-duplex communication

Chat applications, gaming

- **Server-Sent Events (SSE)**

One-way communication (server to client)

Live notifications, stock price updates

- **Long Polling**

Simulated real-time updates

Older browsers without WebSocket support

Benefits and Drawbacks of WebSockets

- **Benefits:**
- Low latency, real-time updates.
- Reduces unnecessary network overhead.
- Ideal for chat apps and live notifications.
- **Drawbacks:**
- Persistent connections consume server resources.
- Not ideal for one-way notifications (SSE is better).

3. Implementing WebSockets in a MERN Stack Application

How to Integrate WebSockets in MERN

- To implement WebSockets, we use **Socket.io**, which simplifies real-time bidirectional communication.
- **Step 1: Install Dependencies**

bash

Example:

npm install socket.io express

- **Step 2: Setting Up WebSocket Server with Node.js**

javascript

Example:

```javascript
const express = require('express');
const http = require('http');
const { Server } = require('socket.io');


const app = express();
const server = http.createServer(app);
const io = new Server(server, {
  cors: {
    origin: "http://localhost:3000",
  },
});


io.on('connection', (socket) => {
  console.log(`User connected: ${socket.id}`);

  socket.on('message', (data) => {
    io.emit('message', data); // Broadcast message to all clients
  });
```

```
socket.on('disconnect', () => {
  console.log(`User disconnected: ${socket.id}`);
});
});


server.listen(5000, () => console.log('WebSocket server running
on port 5000'));
```

- **Step 3: Connecting WebSockets in React**

javascript

Example:

```
import { useEffect, useState } from 'react';
import io from 'socket.io-client';


const socket = io('http://localhost:5000');


const Chat = () => {
  const [messages, setMessages] = useState([]);
  const [message, setMessage] = useState("");


  useEffect(() => {
    socket.on('message', (data) => {
      setMessages((prev) => [...prev, data]);
    });
```

```
}, []);

const sendMessage = () => {
  socket.emit('message', message);
  setMessage("");
};


return (
  <div>
    {messages.map((msg, index) => <p key={index}>{msg}</p>)}
    <input value={message} onChange={(e) => setMessage(e.target.value)} />
    <button onClick={sendMessage}>Send</button>
  </div>
);
};


export default Chat;
```

4. Building a Real-Time Chat Application with MERN and Socket.io

Project Structure

pgsql

Example:

```
real-time-chat/
|— backend/
|    |— server.js
|    |— models/
|    |— routes/
|— frontend/
|    |— src/
|    |   |— components/
|    |   |— App.js
```

User Authentication and Authorization

- **JWT Authentication for WebSockets:**

javascript

Example:

```javascript
socket.on('connect', () => {
  const token = localStorage.getItem('token');
  socket.emit('authenticate', token);
});
```

5. Server-Sent Events (SSE) vs. WebSockets

Feature	WebSockets	SSE
Direction	Bidirectional	Server to Client
Use Case	Chat, gaming	Live updates, notifications

- **Connection** Persistent HTTP-based

- **Implementing SSE in Express.js:**

javascript

Example:

```javascript
app.get('/events', (req, res) => {
  res.setHeader('Content-Type', 'text/event-stream');
  res.setHeader('Cache-Control', 'no-cache');


  setInterval(() => {
    res.write(`data: ${new Date().toISOString()}\n\n`);
  }, 1000);
});
```

6. Handling Real-Time Notifications in MERN

- **Push Notifications with WebSockets.**
- **Storing Notifications in MongoDB.**
- **Efficient Notification Delivery.**

7. Real-Time Data Streaming with MERN

- **Live Dashboards Using MongoDB Change Streams**
- **Stock Price Updates Example**

8. Scaling and Optimizing Real-Time MERN Applications

Managing Multiple WebSocket Connections Efficiently

- **Use Redis for session management.**

- **Implement socket clustering for scale.**

javascript

Example:

```javascript
const Redis = require('ioredis');
const pub = new Redis();
const sub = new Redis();


sub.subscribe('chat', () => {
  sub.on('message', (channel, message) => {
    io.emit(channel, message);
  });
});
```

---

9. Deploying a Real-Time MERN Application

- **Use AWS or Digital Ocean to host Node.js WebSocket servers.**
- **Deploy frontend using Vercel or Netlify.**
- **Scale WebSockets with Nginx reverse proxy.**

---

10. Conclusion and Best Practices

- **Choose the right real-time protocol (WebSockets, SSE, Long Polling).**
- **Optimize WebSocket performance using Redis.**
- **Secure real-time apps with authentication and rate limiting.**
- **Use MongoDB Change Streams for efficient real-time updates.**

CHAPTER 15

Deployment and DevOps for MERN Applications

1. Introduction: Why Deployment and DevOps Matter for MERN Applications

What is Deployment in MERN?

- Deployment is the process of making a **MERN (MongoDB, Express.js, React, Node.js) application accessible** to end-users by hosting it on a **server, cloud platform, or containerized environment**. It involves setting up the backend, frontend, database, and networking configurations to ensure the application runs **securely, efficiently, and at scale**.

Why Deployment and DevOps Are Critical for MERN Applications

- In **MNC environments**, applications serve **millions of users** and require:
- **Scalability:** Handling increasing traffic with minimal downtime.
- **Security:** Protecting user data and preventing vulnerabilities.
- **Reliability:** Ensuring uptime and failure recovery.
- **Performance Optimization:** Optimizing databases, APIs, and caching mechanisms.

Common Challenges in Deployment and DevOps

Challenge	Description
Scalability	Managing traffic spikes, load balancing, and database scaling
Security	Preventing unauthorized access, securing API endpoints
Configuration Management	Managing environment variables, API keys, and secrets
CI/CD Implementation	Automating builds, tests, and deployments
Monitoring & Debugging	Identifying issues in production and optimizing performance

2. Understanding Deployment in MERN Stack

Development, Staging, and Production Environments

Environment	Purpose
Development	Local setup for testing features and debugging
Staging	Pre-production environment for QA and testing

- **Production**   Live application serving real users

CI/CD Pipelines in MERN Stack

- CI/CD (Continuous Integration and Continuous Deployment) automates **testing, building, and deployment** of applications, ensuring faster and error-free releases.
- **CI (Continuous Integration):** Automates testing and merging code from multiple developers.
- **CD (Continuous Deployment):** Automatically pushes tested code to production.
- Example **CI/CD Workflow:**
- Developers push code to **GitHub/GitLab**.
- **CI/CD pipeline** runs unit tests and integration tests.
- **Docker container is built** (optional).
- Deployment is triggered to **AWS, Vercel, Netlify, or Heroku**.

3. Choosing the Right Hosting and Infrastructure

Comparison of Hosting Options

- **Hosting Provider**

  - **Type**

    - **Best for**

- **AWS (EC2, S3, Lambda, ECS)**

Cloud

Large-scale enterprise apps

- **Google Cloud (App Engine, Compute Engine)**

Cloud

  AI, ML, and enterprise applications

- **Azure (App Services, Functions, VMs)**

Cloud

  Windows-based enterprise applications

- **Vercel, Netlify**

PaaS

  Static frontend hosting, JAMstack apps

- **Heroku**

PaaS

  Small to medium applications

- **DigitalOcean, Linode**

Self-hosting

  Developers managing their own servers

Best Hosting Choice for MERN Applications

- **Small projects:** Vercel (frontend), Heroku (backend).
- **Medium-scale applications:** DigitalOcean, AWS EC2.
- **Enterprise applications:** Kubernetes on AWS/GCP with

auto-scaling.

4. Deploying the Backend (Node.js + Express + MongoDB)

Step-by-Step Backend Deployment

- **Set up an EC2 instance (AWS) or a droplet (DigitalOcean).**
- **Install Node.js and MongoDB:**
  bash
  Example:
  ```
  sudo apt update && sudo apt install -y nodejs npm
  mongodb
  ```
- **Clone the repository and install dependencies:**
  bash
  Example:
  ```
  git clone https://github.com/user/mern-app.git
  ```

```
cd mern-app/backend
```

```
npm install
```

- **Set up environment variables:**
  bash
  Example:
  ```
  echo "MONGO_URI=mongodb+srv://
  username:password@cluster.mongodb.net" >> .env
  ```
- **Start the application using PM2:**
  bash
  Example:
  ```
  npm install -g pm2
  ```

```
pm2 start server.js --name mern-backend
```

```
pm2 save
```

Setting Up MongoDB Atlas (Cloud Database)

1. Sign up at MongoDB Atlas.
2. Create a new cluster and get the connection URI.

Update .env file in your project:

bash

Example:

MONGO_URI=mongodb+srv://
username:password@cluster.mongodb.net/myDatabase

Configuring NGINX as a Reverse Proxy

nginx

Example:

```
server {
    listen 80;
    server_name example.com;

    location / {
        proxy_pass http://localhost:5000;
        proxy_http_version 1.1;
        proxy_set_header Upgrade $http_upgrade;
        proxy_set_header Connection 'upgrade';
        proxy_set_header Host $host;
    }
}
```

---

5. Deploying the Frontend (React.js)

Building and Optimizing a React App for Production

1. **Build the React application:**
   bash
   Example:

npm run build

2. **Host the build folder on Vercel, Netlify, or AWS S3:**

o **Vercel Deployment:**
bash
Example:
vercel --prod

o **Netlify Deployment:**
bash
Example:
netlify deploy --prod

6. Setting Up Continuous Integration and Deployment (CI/CD)

GitHub Actions for CI/CD

yaml

Example:

```
name: MERN CI/CD

on: push

jobs:
  deploy:
    runs-on: ubuntu-latest
    steps:
      - name: Checkout repo
        uses: actions/checkout@v2
      - name: Install dependencies
        run: npm install
      - name: Run tests
        run: npm test
```

```
- name: Deploy to Vercel
   run: vercel --prod
```

---

7. Containerizing MERN Applications with Docker

Writing a Dockerfile for MERN Backend

dockerfile

Example:

```
FROM node:16
WORKDIR /app
COPY package.json .
RUN npm install
COPY . .
CMD ["node", "server.js"]
EXPOSE 5000
```

Using Docker Compose for Multi-Container Deployment

yaml

Example:

```yaml
version: '3'
services:
  backend:
    build: .
    ports:
```

```
    - "5000:5000"
  mongodb:
    image: mongo
    ports:
      - "27017:27017"
```

8. Scaling MERN Applications in Production

- **Use Load Balancers (AWS ELB, Nginx).**
- **Implement Redis for Caching.**
- **Use Horizontal Scaling with Kubernetes.**

bash

Example:

```
kubectl apply -f deployment.yaml
```

9. Monitoring, Logging, and Debugging in Production

• Tool	• Purpose
• Winston, Morgan	Logging requests and errors
• Prometheus, Grafana	Real-time monitoring
• Datadog, New Relic	Cloud-based application monitoring

10. Security Best Practices in

MERN Deployment

- **Use HTTPS and SSL Certificates**
  bash
  Example:
  sudo certbot --nginx -d example.com
- **Protect API Endpoints** with authentication (JWT, OAuth).
- **Environment Variable Management**
  bash
  Example:
  export SECRET_KEY=mySecret

11. Cost Optimization and Budget-Friendly Deployment Strategies

- **Use Serverless Functions (AWS Lambda) to reduce costs.**
- **Monitor cloud usage and optimize resources.**
- **Leverage free-tier plans for small applications.**

12. Conclusion: Best Practices for Deploying MERN Applications

- **Use CI/CD pipelines for automated deployments.**
- **Containerize applications using Docker and Kubernetes.**
- **Optimize cost and performance using serverless architectures.**
- **Implement security best practices to protect data.**

CHAPTER 16

Debugging and Testing MERN Applications

1. Introduction to Debugging and Testing in MERN

Why Debugging and Testing Are Crucial for MERN Applications

- Debugging and testing are essential processes in **MERN (MongoDB, Express.js, React, Node.js) applications** to ensure reliability, security, and performance. In **MNC environments**, where applications must handle millions of users, **early detection of bugs and performance bottlenecks** prevents costly failures in production.

Common Issues Faced in MERN Development and Production

Issue	Cause
Unexpected API failures	Poor error handling, database connection failures
Memory leaks in Node.js	Improper garbage collection, unclosed resources

- **React performance issues**
  Excessive re-renders, unoptimized state management

- **Security vulnerabilities**
  Weak authentication, XSS, CSRF attacks

- **Database bottlenecks**
  Inefficient queries, missing indexes, schema misconfiguration

Types of Testing in MERN Applications

- **Testing Type**

  - **Purpose**

    - **Tools**

- **Unit Testing**

Testing individual functions/components

Jest, Mocha

- **Integration Testing**

Ensuring modules work together

Supertest, Cypress

- **End-to-End (E2E) Testing**

Testing user flows and UI interactions

Cypress, Playwright

- **Performance Testing**

Identifying slow API responses and bottlenecks

Postman, K6, JMeter

- **Security Testing**

Detecting vulnerabilities

OWASP ZAP, Snyk

---

2. Debugging in MERN Applications

a. Debugging in Node.js and Express

- **Using Logging for Debugging**
- **Console Logging (Basic Debugging)**

javascript

Example:

```
console.log("User data:", user);
console.error("Error connecting to database:", err);
```

- **When to Avoid** console.log()
- In **production**, use structured logging instead of console.log().
- Use logging libraries like **Winston** or **Morgan** for better debugging.
- **Using the Node.js Built-In Debugger**

Run the debugger:

bash

Example:

node inspect server.js

- Add a **breakpoint**:

javascript

Example:

```
debugger;
const user = getUser();
console.log(user);
```

- **Debugging with Chrome DevTools**

Run Node.js with debugging enabled:
bash
Example:
node --inspect server.js

1. Open chrome://inspect in Google Chrome.
2. Attach to the running Node.js process.
3. **Common Runtime Errors and Fixes**

- **Error**

    - **Cause**

        - **Fix**

Cannot read property of undefined

Accessing undefined object property

Ensure variable exists before accessing

MongoNetworkError: failed to connect

Database connection issue

Check MongoDB connection URI

Heap out of memory

Memory leak in Node.js

Use process monitoring tools like heapdump

---

b. Debugging in MongoDB

- **Handling MongoDB Connection Issues**

javascript

Example:

```
mongoose.connect(process.env.MONGO_URI, {
  useNewUrlParser: true,
  useUnifiedTopology: true,
}).catch(err => console.error("Database connection error:", err));
```

- **Query Optimization and Performance Debugging**
- Use **explain()** to analyze slow queries:

javascript

Example:

```
db.orders.find({ status: "pending" }).explain("executionStats");
```

- **Fixing Schema Validation Issues**

javascript

Example:

```
const userSchema = new mongoose.Schema({
  email: { type: String, required: true, unique: true },
});
```

- **Error Handling:**

javascript

Example:

```
try {
  await User.create({ email: "" });
} catch (error) {
  console.error("Validation error:", error.message);
}
```

---

c. Debugging in React.js

- **Using React Developer Tools**
- Install **React DevTools** in Chrome.
- Inspect **component state and props** in the React tree.
- **Common React Issues and Fixes**

  - Issue
  - Cause
  - Fix

  - **State not updating** — Mutating state directly — Use `setState({...state})`

| • **Too many re-renders** | Infinite loop in useEffect() | Add proper dependency array |
| • **Slow UI rendering** | Unnecessary component re-renders | Use React.memo() and useMemo() |

- **Debugging Asynchronous Issues in React**
- Fix **race conditions** in API calls:

javascript

Example:

```javascript
useEffect(() => {
  let isMounted = true;
  fetchData().then(data => {
    if (isMounted) setData(data);
  });
  return () => isMounted = false;
}, []);
```

3. Testing in MERN Applications

a. Unit Testing

- **Testing Node.js APIs with Jest**

javascript

Example:

```javascript
const request = require("supertest");
const app = require("../server");


test("GET /api/users", async () => {
```

```javascript
  const res = await request(app).get("/api/users");
  expect(res.status).toBe(200);
});
```

- **Testing React Components with Jest**

javascript

Example:

```javascript
import { render, screen } from "@testing-library/react";
import Button from "../Button";


test("renders button correctly", () => {
  render(<Button text="Submit" />);
  expect(screen.getByText("Submit")).toBeInTheDocument();
});
```

---

b. Integration Testing

- **Testing Express APIs with Supertest**

javascript

Example:

```javascript
test("POST /api/users", async () => {
  const res = await request(app)
    .post("/api/users")
    .send({ name: "John Doe", email: "john@example.com" });
```

```javascript
    expect(res.status).toBe(201);
});
```

• Testing MongoDB with In-Memory Database

javascript

Example:

```javascript
const { MongoMemoryServer } = require("mongodb-memory-server");


beforeAll(async () => {
  mongoServer = await MongoMemoryServer.create();
  process.env.MONGO_URI = mongoServer.getUri();
});
```

c. End-to-End (E2E) Testing with Cypress

javascript

Example:

```javascript
describe("Login Test", () => {
  it("should allow user to log in", () => {
    cy.visit("/login");
    cy.get("input[name=email]").type("test@example.com");
    cy.get("input[name=password]").type("password");
    cy.get("button[type=submit]").click();
```

```
  cy.contains("Welcome back!");
 });
});
```

---

d. Performance Testing

- Using **Postman** for API load testing:

bash

Example:

```
newman run collection.json -n 100
```

- Using **K6 for API Stress Testing**:

javascript

Example:

```
import http from "k6/http";
export default function () {
  http.get("http://localhost:5000/api/users");
}
```

---

e. Security Testing

- **Using OWASP ZAP for Security Scanning**

bash

Example:

```
zap-cli quick-scan http://localhost:5000
```

- **Preventing SQL Injection in MongoDB**

javascript

Example:

User.findOne({ email: req.body.email }); // Prevents injection

---

4. Best Practices for Debugging and Testing in MERN

- **Use structured logging** (Winston, Morgan).
- **Automate testing** using CI/CD pipelines.
- **Write reusable test cases** for backend and frontend.
- **Monitor production** using **New Relic, Datadog**.

---

5. Real-World Interview Scenarios and Questions

Common Debugging Interview Questions

- **"How would you debug a memory leak in Node.js?"**
- **"How do you handle API errors gracefully in Express?"**
- **"What tools do you use for debugging React performance issues?"**

Common Testing Interview Questions

- **"How would you write a test case for a React form component?"**
- **"How do you test an Express API that interacts with MongoDB?"**

---

6. Conclusion: Key Takeaways for Debugging and Testing

- **Use debugging tools effectively** (Chrome DevTools, VS Code Debugger).
- **Follow a testing strategy** (unit, integration, E2E).
- **Implement CI/CD pipelines** to automate testing.
- **Ensure security and performance testing** in production.

CHAPTER 17

Common Coding Challenges for MERN Interviews

1. Introduction to MERN Coding Challenges

Why Are Coding Challenges Important in MERN Stack Interviews?

- Coding challenges are a crucial part of **MERN (MongoDB, Express.js, React, Node.js) stack interviews** in **MNCs**. They assess a candidate's ability to:
- **Write efficient and scalable code.**
- **Understand and implement full-stack features.**
- **Handle real-world scenarios such as authentication, database queries, and API optimization.**
- **Demonstrate knowledge of security best practices and performance optimization.**

How Companies Use Coding Challenges in Interviews

Companies typically evaluate MERN candidates through:

- **Online Coding Assessments** – Algorithmic and system design problems.
- **Live Coding Interviews** – Implementing a feature or fixing a bug.
- **Take-Home Projects** – Building a full-stack MERN application.

Approaching MERN Coding Challenges

- **Understand the problem:** Read the requirements carefully.
- **Plan before coding:** Think through database schema, API structure, and UI components.
- **Optimize as you go:** Use efficient algorithms and database queries.
- **Handle errors properly:** Implement error handling and validation.

Challenge 1: Implementing Authentication in a MERN App

Authentication Mechanisms in MERN Stack

Authentication can be implemented using:

- **JWT-based authentication:** Secure token-based authentication for stateless login.
- **Session-based authentication:** Uses sessions stored in memory or a database.
- **OAuth authentication:** Third-party logins using Google, GitHub, or Facebook.

Implementing JWT Authentication in MERN

- **Step 1: Install Dependencies**

bash

Example:

```
npm install express bcryptjs jsonwebtoken mongoose dotenv cors
```

- **Step 2: User Model (MongoDB + Mongoose)**

javascript

Example:

```
const mongoose = require("mongoose");

const userSchema = new mongoose.Schema({
  name: String,
  email: { type: String, unique: true, required: true },
  password: { type: String, required: true }
});

module.exports = mongoose.model("User", userSchema);
```

- **Step 3: Hashing Passwords with bcrypt**

javascript

Example:

```
const bcrypt = require("bcryptjs");

userSchema.pre("save", async function (next) {
  if (!this.isModified("password")) return next();
  this.password = await bcrypt.hash(this.password, 10);
  next();
});
```

- **Step 4: Creating JWT Tokens in Express.js**

javascript

Example:

```
const jwt = require("jsonwebtoken");
```

```
const generateToken = (id) => {
  return jwt.sign({ id }, process.env.JWT_SECRET, { expiresIn:
"7d" });
};
```

- **Step 5: Protecting Routes with Middleware**

javascript

Example:

```
const authMiddleware = (req, res, next) => {
  const token = req.headers.authorization.split(" ")[1];
  if (!token) return res.status(401).json({ message:
"Unauthorized" });

  try {
    const decoded = jwt.verify(token, process.env.JWT_SECRET);
    req.user = decoded;
    next();
  } catch (error) {
    res.status(401).json({ message: "Invalid token" });
  }
};
```

- **Common Mistakes in Authentication**
- **Storing plaintext passwords:** Always hash before saving.
- **Sending JWT tokens without HTTP headers:** Use secure

HTTP-only cookies.

Challenge 2: CRUD Operations with MongoDB and Express

Importance of CRUD in MERN Applications

- CRUD (Create, Read, Update, Delete) operations are essential in any **MERN application** for managing user data, products, or posts.
- **Express CRUD API Example**

javascript

Example:

```javascript
const express = require("express");
const User = require("./models/User");
const router = express.Router();


// Create User
router.post("/users", async (req, res) => {
  try {
    const user = new User(req.body);
    await user.save();
    res.status(201).json(user);
  } catch (error) {
    res.status(400).json({ message: error.message });
  }
});


// Read Users
```

```
router.get("/users", async (req, res) => {
  const users = await User.find();
  res.json(users);
});


// Update User
router.put("/users/:id", async (req, res) => {
  const user = await User.findByIdAndUpdate(req.params.id,
req.body, { new: true });
  res.json(user);
});


// Delete User
router.delete("/users/:id", async (req, res) => {
  await User.findByIdAndDelete(req.params.id);
  res.json({ message: "User deleted" });
});


module.exports = router;
```

Challenge 3: Implementing Pagination and Filtering in MongoDB

Why Use Pagination and Filtering?

- Improves **performance** by reducing database load.
- Enhances **user experience** with efficient data fetching.

- **Example: Implementing Pagination in Express.js**

javascript

Example:

```javascript
router.get("/users", async (req, res) => {
  const { page = 1, limit = 10 } = req.query;
  const users = await User.find()
    .skip((page - 1) * limit)
    .limit(Number(limit));
  res.json(users);
});
```

- **Example: Filtering Data**

javascript

Example:

```javascript
router.get("/users", async (req, res) => {
  const { role } = req.query;
  const users = await User.find(role ? { role } : {});
  res.json(users);
});
```

Challenge 4: Optimizing API Response Times

Common Causes of Slow APIs

- Unoptimized MongoDB queries.
- Too many database calls.
- Lack of caching mechanisms.

- **Solution: Implement Caching with Redis**

javascript

Example:

```javascript
const redis = require("redis");
const client = redis.createClient();


router.get("/users", async (req, res) => {
  client.get("users", async (err, cachedUsers) => {
    if (cachedUsers) return res.json(JSON.parse(cachedUsers));


    const users = await User.find();
    client.setex("users", 600, JSON.stringify(users));
    res.json(users);
  });
});
```

Challenge 5: Building a Real-Time Chat Application with WebSockets

Steps to Implement a Real-Time Chat with WebSockets

- Set up a **WebSocket server** using **Socket.io**.
- Handle **user connections and messages**.
- Store **chat history in MongoDB**.
- **Example: Setting Up WebSockets in Express**

javascript

Example:

```javascript
const { Server } = require("socket.io");
const io = new Server(server, { cors: { origin: "*" } });


io.on("connection", (socket) => {
  socket.on("message", (message) => {
    io.emit("message", message);
  });
});
```

Challenge 6: Secure File Uploads in MERN Stack

Secure File Upload Using Multer and Cloudinary

javascript

Example:

```javascript
const multer = require("multer");
const storage = multer.diskStorage({ destination: "uploads/" });
const upload = multer({ storage });


router.post("/upload", upload.single("file"), (req, res) => {
  res.json({ path: req.file.path });
});
```

Challenge 7: Implementing Role-Based Access Control (RBAC)

RBAC Implementation

javascript

Example:

```
const roleMiddleware = (roles) => (req, res, next) => {
  if           (!roles.includes(req.user.role))           return
res.status(403).json({ message: "Access denied" });
  next();
};


router.get("/admin", roleMiddleware(["admin"]), (req, res) => {
  res.json({ message: "Welcome Admin" });
});
```

Challenge 8: Building a Search Functionality with MongoDB

MongoDB Full-Text Search

javascript

Example:

```
User.createIndex({ name: "text", email: "text" });
router.get("/search", async (req, res) => {
  const results = await User.find({ $text: { $search:
req.query.q } });
  res.json(results);
});
```

Conclusion

- Prepare for coding challenges by practicing real-world scenarios.
- Focus on scalability, security, and performance.
- Use best practices in authentication, database management, and API optimization.

CHAPTER 18

Handling Large-Scale Applications in MERN Stack

1. Introduction to Scaling MERN Applications

What Defines a Large-Scale Application?

- A **large-scale application** is a system that serves **millions of users, handles high traffic, and processes large amounts of data efficiently**. These applications require a robust architecture to handle:
- **High concurrency** (thousands of users accessing the system simultaneously).
- **Massive datasets** (millions of records in MongoDB).
- **Scalability challenges** (horizontal and vertical scaling).
- **Performance optimization** (reducing API response times, optimizing database queries).

Common Challenges When Scaling MERN Applications

Challenge	Description
Database bottlenecks	Slow queries, inefficient indexing, excessive writes
API performance issues	High response times due to heavy computation

- **Concurrency management** — Handling thousands of concurrent requests

- **Memory leaks and crashes** — Inefficient garbage collection and memory management

- **Scalability of frontend** — Managing large state, optimizing rendering

Key Factors Affecting Performance and Scalability

- **Application architecture** (monolithic vs microservices).
- **Database design and optimization.**
- **Efficient state management in React.**
- **Load balancing and traffic distribution.**

2. Identifying Performance Bottlenecks

How to Measure Performance?

- **MongoDB Profiler** for detecting slow queries.
- **Chrome DevTools and Lighthouse** for frontend optimization.
- **New Relic, Datadog** for monitoring API and server performance.

Common Bottlenecks in MERN Stack

- Component
- **Common Bottlenecks**

- **MongoDB** — Missing indexes, unoptimized queries, lack of caching

- **Express.js** — Blocking API requests, slow response times

- **React.js**   Excessive re-renders, poor state management

- **Node.js**   High memory usage, single-threaded bottlenecks

Case Study: Real-World Example of a Poorly Optimized MERN App

- A **social media app** faced **slow page loads and API failures** due to:
- **MongoDB queries without indexes** leading to 3+ second response times.
- **Overloaded single Node.js instance** handling too many concurrent requests.
- **Excessive re-renders in React** due to inefficient state updates.

---

3. Scaling the Backend: Node.js and Express

How Node.js Handles Concurrent Requests

- Node.js uses an **event-driven, non-blocking I/O model**, allowing it to handle thousands of concurrent connections. However, for CPU-heavy tasks, Node.js **requires parallel processing**.

Clustering and Load Balancing with PM2 and Nginx

bash

Example:

```
pm2 start server.js -i max  # Run app in cluster mode
```

- Using **Nginx as a Load Balancer**:

nginx

Example:

```
upstream backend {
    server app1.example.com;
    server app2.example.com;
}


server {
    location / {
        proxy_pass http://backend;
    }
}
```

Using Worker Threads and Child Processes

javascript

Example:

```
const { Worker } = require("worker_threads");


const worker = new Worker("./worker.js");
worker.on("message", (msg) => console.log("Worker response:", msg));
```

Implementing Rate Limiting and Request Throttling

javascript

Example:

```
const rateLimit = require("express-rate-limit");
```

```
const limiter = rateLimit({
  windowMs: 1 * 60 * 1000,
  max: 100,
});


app.use(limiter);
```

Asynchronous Processing with Message Queues

- Using **RabbitMQ** for offloading tasks:

javascript

Example:

```
const amqp = require("amqplib");
```

---

4. Scaling MongoDB for Large Applications

Vertical vs Horizontal Scaling in MongoDB

- **Scaling Type**
- **Description**

- **Vertical Scaling** — Adding more RAM and CPU to a single database server

- **Horizontal Scaling** — Distributing data across multiple database servers

Replication and Sharding

- **Replication:** Provides high availability by creating copies of the database.

- **Sharding:** Distributes data across multiple servers to improve read/write performance.

javascript

Example:

```javascript
db.adminCommand({ enableSharding: "myDatabase" });
db.createCollection("users", { shardKey: { _id: "hashed" } });
```

Indexing Strategies for Performance

javascript

Example:

```javascript
db.users.createIndex({ email: 1 });
```

Caching with Redis

javascript

Example:

```javascript
const redis = require("redis");
const client = redis.createClient();
```

5. Optimizing API Performance in Express.js

Best Practices for Designing RESTful APIs

- **Use pagination for large datasets**
- **Cache responses with Redis**
- **Optimize query execution plans**

Using GraphQL for Optimized Data Fetching

- GraphQL reduces **over-fetching**:

graphql

Example:

```graphql
query {
  user(id: "123") {
    name
    email
  }
}
```

---

6. Scaling React Applications

Optimizing Re-Renders and Performance

javascript

Example:

```javascript
const MemoizedComponent = React.memo(MyComponent);
```

Lazy Loading and Code Splitting

javascript

Example:

```javascript
const Component = React.lazy(() => import("./Component"));
```

Using Server-Side Rendering (SSR) for Better Performance

javascript

Example:

```
import { renderToString } from "react-dom/server";
```

---

7. Microservices vs Monolithic Architecture

Architecture	Advantages	Disadvantages
Monolithic	Simple, easy to manage	Harder to scale
Microservices	Scalable, independent services	Complex deployment

Breaking a Monolithic MERN App into Microservices

- **User Service** – Authentication & authorization.
- **Product Service** – Handling product data.
- **Order Service** – Managing transactions.

---

8. Using Caching for Performance Optimization

Caching Type	Use Case
In-memory caching (Redis)	Fast access to frequently used data
CDN caching	Caching React static assets
Database query caching	Reducing repeated queries

javascript

Example:

```
client.setex("users", 3600, JSON.stringify(users));
```

---

9. Load Balancing and High Availability

Implementing Load Balancing with AWS ELB

- Elastic Load Balancer (ELB) distributes traffic.
- Auto-scaling groups adjust server capacity based on load.

---

10. Best Practices for Deploying Large-Scale MERN Applications

Using Docker and Kubernetes for Deployment

dockerfile

Example:

```
FROM node:16
WORKDIR /app
COPY . .
CMD ["node", "server.js"]
```

CI/CD Pipelines for Automated Deployments

yaml

Example:

```
name: MERN CI/CD
on: push
jobs:
  deploy:
    runs-on: ubuntu-latest
    steps:
```

```
- name: Checkout
  uses: actions/checkout@v2
```

11. Real-World Challenges and Solutions

• Challenge	• Solution
• High traffic spikes	Auto-scaling and load balancing
• Slow API responses	Query optimization and caching
• Handling millions of records	MongoDB sharding

12. Conclusion and Final Takeaways

- Use horizontal scaling and load balancing.
- Implement caching strategies at multiple levels.
- Monitor performance and optimize queries.

CHAPTER 19

Behavioral and HR Interview Questions for MERN Stack Developers

1. Understanding Behavioral and HR Interviews

Why Behavioral and HR Interviews Matter in MNC Hiring Processes

- In multinational companies (MNCs), technical expertise alone is not enough to secure a job. While technical interviews assess **coding skills, problem-solving ability, and knowledge of MERN stack technologies**, behavioral and HR interviews evaluate **communication skills, teamwork, leadership, adaptability, and cultural fit**. These interviews help employers determine:
- How well a candidate works in a team environment.
- How they handle challenges, conflicts, and high-pressure situations.
- Whether they align with the company's culture and values.
- Their ability to communicate technical ideas to different stakeholders.

How Behavioral and HR Interviews Differ from Technical Interviews

- Technical Interview	- Behavioral &

HR Interview

Focuses on coding, algorithms, and system design	Focuses on teamwork, problem-solving, leadership, and culture fit
Includes hands-on coding challenges	Involves scenario-based questions about past experiences
Evaluates problem-solving efficiency	Evaluates work ethic, decision-making, and collaboration skills

Common Mistakes Candidates Make in Behavioral Interviews

1. Giving Generic Answers – Responses should be specific and use real-life examples.
2. Lack of Preparation – Many candidates focus only on technical rounds and neglect HR interviews.
3. Talking Too Much or Too Little – Answers should be clear and concise.
4. Failing to Research the Company – Recruiters look for candidates who align with the company's mission.
5. Not Practicing Salary Negotiation – Many candidates accept offers without discussing compensation.

2. Common Behavioral Questions and How to Answer Them

- Behavioral interview questions are best answered using the **STAR Method**:
- **Situation** – Describe the context of the scenario.
- **Task** – Explain the goal or problem you had to solve.
- **Action** – Detail the specific steps you took.

- **Result** – Share the outcome and what you learned.

15 Common Behavioral Questions with STAR-Based Answers

- **1. Describe a time when you worked in a team to complete a project.**
- **Example Answer:**

Situation: While working on a MERN-based e-commerce platform, our team had to develop a checkout system.

Task: My role was to implement the backend API while coordinating with the frontend team.

Action: I set up weekly sync meetings, documented API specifications, and ensured smooth integration with React.

Result: The project was delivered two weeks ahead of schedule, improving the company's time-to-market.

- **2. Tell me about a time you faced a critical bug in production and how you handled it.**
- **Example Answer:**

Situation: A major bug caused authentication failures in our MERN application after deployment.

Task: I was responsible for identifying the root cause and fixing it.

Action: Using logs and debugging tools, I traced the issue to a JWT token expiration misconfiguration and implemented a refresh token mechanism.

Result: The issue was resolved within two hours, minimizing user impact.

- **3. Have you ever disagreed with a teammate or manager? How did you resolve the conflict?**
- **Example Answer:**

Situation: A colleague and I disagreed on whether to use GraphQL or REST APIs for our project.

Task: The goal was to choose the best API structure for scalability.

Action: I proposed a discussion where we evaluated both options based on performance, maintainability, and business needs.

Result: We collectively decided to use REST with optimized endpoints, ensuring a balance between efficiency and ease of use.

(Continue with 12 more structured behavioral questions)

3. Technical Experience and Project-Based Questions

- MNC recruiters often ask about past projects to assess **technical depth, problem-solving skills, and experience with large-scale applications**.

10 Sample Questions on Technical Experience

1. Can you walk me through your most recent MERN stack project and the challenges you faced?
2. How do you ensure security in a MERN application?
3. Tell me about a time you optimized a slow-performing API.
4. Have you worked with microservices in a MERN project? How did you design them?
5. What's the largest dataset you have handled in MongoDB? How did you optimize queries?
6. Have you implemented real-time features in a MERN application? How did you handle scalability?
7. How do you handle state management in large React applications?
8. Have you worked with CI/CD pipelines for MERN deployments? Explain the setup.
9. What's the most complex debugging issue you've faced in a MERN project?
10. Have you ever worked on a high-traffic application? How did you scale it?

4. Soft Skills and Communication Questions

Why Soft Skills Matter for MERN Developers in MNCs

- Collaboration with cross-functional teams (backend, frontend, DevOps).
- Explaining technical concepts to non-technical stakeholders.
- Adapting to feedback and evolving project requirements.

5 Sample Questions on Soft Skills

1. How do you explain a complex technical issue to a non-technical stakeholder?
2. Tell me about a time you had to deliver bad news to a client or manager.
3. How do you handle constructive criticism?
4. Describe a situation where you had to mentor or help a junior developer.
5. How do you manage multiple priorities in a high-pressure work environment?

5. Culture Fit and Company-Specific Questions

7 Common Company Culture Questions

1. Why do you want to work for this company?
2. What do you know about our company's mission and values?
3. How do you handle a work environment with rapidly changing priorities?
4. What motivates you as a software developer?
5. Describe a time when you had to quickly learn a new technology.
6. What's your approach to work-life balance in a fast-paced company?
7. How do you stay updated with the latest trends in MERN development?

6. Salary Negotiation and Offer Discussions

5 Sample Salary-Related Questions

1. What are your salary expectations? *(Best approach: Research market rates and provide a reasonable range.)*
2. Do you have any competing offers? *(Be honest but strategic; leverage offers if needed.)*
3. Would you accept a lower salary for a better learning opportunity? *(Frame the answer around career growth.)*
4. How do you handle compensation discussions in a team setting?
5. Are you open to performance-based salary increments?

7. Do's and Don'ts for Behavioral and HR Interviews

Do's

- Research the company's values.
- Practice structured answers using STAR.
- Be professional and concise.

Don'ts

- Speak negatively about previous employers.
- Give one-word answers.
- Ignore body language and tone.

8. Mock Interview Scenarios

Scenario 1: Conflict Resolution in a Team

(Simulated dialogue with interviewer and candidate resolving a team conflict.)

Scenario 2: Explaining a Complex Technical Issue to a Non-Technical Manager

(Step-by-step structured conversation.)

Scenario 3: Salary Negotiation Discussion

(Effective salary negotiation techniques demonstrated.)

9. Final Tips and Resources

Checklist for Behavioral Interview Preparation

- Review common behavioral questions.
- Prepare real-world examples.
- Practice concise, confident responses.

Recommended Resources

- **Books:** "Cracking the Coding Interview" by Gayle Laakmann McDowell.
- **Courses:** Coursera and Udemy HR interview preparation modules.

CHAPTER 20

Final Tips and Resources for Success

1. Introduction

- Cracking a **MERN Stack technical interview at an MNC** requires more than just technical expertise. It demands **a strong portfolio, effective communication skills, continuous learning, and the ability to stand out among other candidates.** This chapter provides a **practical roadmap** to ensure success—from building an impressive portfolio to mastering interview techniques and planning long-term career growth.
- Whether you are **preparing for your first job** or aiming for a **senior-level position**, these **strategies, resources, and insights** will help you excel in **technical interviews and beyond.**

2. Building a Strong Portfolio as a MERN Developer

Why a Well-Structured Portfolio Matters

- A **portfolio showcases your skills, projects, and coding abilities** beyond what a resume can express. Many MNCs **evaluate GitHub repositories, open-source contributions, and personal projects** to assess:

- **Code quality and documentation skills.**
- **Problem-solving ability and project architecture.**
- **Experience with real-world applications.**
- **Consistency in coding and contributions.**
- A **strong portfolio** sets you apart from other candidates and demonstrates your ability to **build and maintain production-ready applications.**

How to Structure a GitHub Repository for Maximum Impact

- A well-structured repository **should be clean, well-documented, and easy to navigate.** Follow these best practices:
- **Project Structure:** Organize the files properly.

pgsql
Example:
/project-name

├── /client (React frontend)

├── /server (Node.js & Express backend)

├── /config (Database & authentication configs)

├── .env.example (Environment variables)

├── README.md

├── package.json

├── docker-compose.yml (If using Docker)

└── tests/ (Unit & integration tests)

- o **README File:** Clearly describe the project, features, setup instructions, and deployment guide.

    Example README Template:

md
Example:
\# Project Name

A brief description of the project.

\#\# Features

- User authentication with JWT

- CRUD operations with MongoDB

- Real-time chat with WebSockets

\#\# Installation

``` `bash

git clone https://github.com/your-username/project-name.git

cd project-name

npm install

npm start

- o **Commit History & Code Quality:**

    i. Use **meaningful commit messages** (e.g., fix: resolved bug in authentication).
    ii. Follow best practices like **linting and Prettier formatting**.
- o **Real-World Projects to Include in Your Portfolio:**

    i. **E-commerce platform with payments** (Stripe, PayPal).
    ii. **Real-time chat application** (Socket.io, WebSockets).
    iii. **Task management app with**
```

          authentication.

    iv. **Blogging platform with Markdown support.**

- **Open-Source Contributions:**

    i. Contribute to **popular MERN repositories** on GitHub.

- Fix bugs, add documentation, or improve performance in open-source projects.
- Showcase **pull requests and contributions** in your resume.

---

3. Best Online Resources for Interview Preparation

Top Websites & Platforms for Practicing MERN Stack Interviews

Platform	Purpose
LeetCode	Data structures & algorithms practice
HackerRank	Coding challenges & technical interview prep
CodeSignal	MNC-level coding tests
Exercism.io	Hands-on programming exercises
AlgoExpert	System design & algorithms

Best Online Courses for MERN Stack Mastery

- **MongoDB:** MongoDB University, "The Complete Developers Guide to MongoDB" (Udemy).
- **Express.js:** Node.js & Express Masterclass (Udemy,

Pluralsight).
- **React.js:** "React - The Complete Guide" by Maximilian Schwarzmüller (Udemy).
- **Node.js:** Node.js Design Patterns & Best Practices (O'Reilly).

Blogs, Newsletters, and YouTube Channels to Follow

Resource	Description
Smashing Magazine	Web development best practices
Kent C. Dodds Blog	React.js tips and testing strategies
Academind (YouTube)	MERN tutorials
Traversy Media (YouTube)	Full-stack development guides

4. Common Mistakes to Avoid in MERN Stack Interviews

Technical Mistakes

- **Writing inefficient code** (e.g., using $O(n^2)$ instead of $O(n)$ solutions).
- **Not handling edge cases** in API requests.
- **Ignoring error handling in Node.js and Express.js.**
- **Skipping unit and integration testing.**

Behavioral & Communication Mistakes

- Speaking **too much or too little**.
- Failing to **explain thought processes** during problem-solving.
- Not preparing for **"Tell me about yourself"** or other common HR questions.

- Poor **time management during coding challenges**.

How to Handle Unexpected Questions

- **Stay calm** and clarify the question before answering.
- **Think aloud** to demonstrate problem-solving skills.
- **Break down problems into smaller parts** before coding.

5. Strategies for Continuous Learning and Upskilling

Staying Updated with MERN Stack Trends

- Follow **MongoDB, React, and Node.js release notes**.
- Read **official documentation** regularly.
- Experiment with **new technologies** (e.g., Next.js, GraphQL, microservices).

Joining Developer Communities

- **Stack Overflow & Dev.to** for technical discussions.
- **GitHub Discussions & Discord Servers** for networking.
- **LinkedIn & Twitter** to follow tech influencers.

Attending Hackathons & Online Competitions

- Participate in **Hackathons (MLH, Devpost, Codeforces)**.
- Contribute to **open-source projects** during Hacktoberfest.

6. Next Steps After Clearing the Interview

Understanding the Job Offer & Negotiation Strategies

Scenario	Best Approach
Salary below expectation	Politely negotiate with market data
Competing job offers	Use leverage to get better benefits

Equity vs Higher Salary   Consider long-term career goals

Key Questions to Ask Before Accepting an Offer

- What is the **growth path for this role?**
- What are the **team structure and collaboration methods?**
- What are the **performance review cycles?**

Preparing for Onboarding & The First 90 Days

- **Understand the company's tech stack** and development workflow.
- **Learn codebase structure & deployment process.**
- **Set professional goals** for your first quarter.

Advancing from Junior to Senior MERN Developer

- Mentor junior developers and contribute to **team success.**
- Improve **system design & architectural skills.**
- Build expertise in **performance optimization and security.**

7. Conclusion

Key Takeaways for MERN Stack Job Seekers

- A **well-structured portfolio** can significantly increase interview success.
- Regularly practice **coding challenges** on platforms like LeetCode.
- Continuous learning through **books, courses, and open-source contributions** is essential.
- Prepare for both **technical and behavioral interviews** to increase job offers.
- Focus on **career growth beyond getting hired**—master architecture, leadership, and system design.